HELL IS NOT MY HOME

MARY SUE MILLER

HELL IS NOT MY HOME

All scripture quotations are taken from the King James Version of the Bible.

This novel is a fiction. Any names, characters, places and incidents are coincidental.

ISBN-13: 978-0692496138

DEDICATION

I dedicate this book to my husband, Thomas Miller, Jr., my parents, Rev. John Henry Parker, and Janie Novella Parker, and my brother James David Parker. Even though my mother was the only one who had knowledge that I was writing this book, I know my husband, father and brother would have been grateful to know that my dream came true. I will never forget my mother telling me, "I want you to go ahead and publish that book." I honor my mother and her heartfelt words as I have now published my book.

HELL IS NOT MY HOME

MARY SUE MILLER

CONTENTS

ACKNOWLEDGEMENTS

First, I thank God, who is the head of my life and I thank Him for giving me the wisdom and knowledge to write this book. Before I wrote this book, I prayed, "God, you be the author and I will be the writer." James 1:5 says, "If any of you lack wisdom, let him ask of God, that giveth to all men liberally, and upbraideth not; and it shall be given him."

To my only child, Dr. Diandrea McCotter, I thank you so much for believing in me from day one. You encouraged me to persevere when I was about to give up. I thank you for taking me back and forth to Creative Writing class every week. You hung in there with me. Your guidance, support and love will always be with me. I love you and I will never forget how hard you worked and prayed with me.

To my niece, Cherice Artis, you hung in there with me from the beginning until the end. At times, I felt like you were working harder that I. I love you so much. I will never forget your time and support and I thank you for all your endeavors. You reminded me that I could do all things through Christ that strengthens me. You never let me down when I needed a lift up. I owe you a BIG THANK YOU!

To my editor, Frances Blount, I thank you for the awesome job you have done. I will never forget your patience and thoughtfulness. Just be ready for my next book! I pray God will continue to bless you.

To my siblings, Retha Roach, Sarah Connor, and Bishop Charles Parker, I thank you so much for your love and support. Also, to the rest of my family, although I cannot thank you all by name here, please know that I thank you from the bottom of my heart.

To John Landrine, The Christian's Writer, I thank you for assisting me with publishing my book. You did an awesome job and I pray that God will continue to elevate you higher and higher in all your endeavors.

To my Creative Writing class at Pitt Community College, I thank you for your critiques and support. A special thanks to my instructor, Ms. Patsy O'Leary.

To the Greenville Guild, I thank you for allowing me to join your writing group. All of your valuable advice and support have finally paid off. A special thanks to Mr. Bob Graham for accepting me into the group.

Last, but not least, I like to thank the Daughters of Glory Book Club and everyone for your love, confidence and support and may God Bless every one of you.

CHAPTER ONE

My family was wondering why I had been unconscious for so long. Little they knew my spirit had actually left from my body and was floating away into another world. I was trying to fight back, but it was useless. The force was too intense. Desperation was upon me. I could hear myself cry out for help, but no one else could hear me. Movement was impossible, and no sound escaped my lips.

Suddenly, I stopped floating, and my arms, as if they had a mind of their own, lifted majestically, like the wings of an eagle. I soared into a vertical position, descending to my destination. Closing my eyes, I could hear the sound of the wind and feel the pressure against my cheeks. The dry air stripped my long salt and pepper hair of its natural curls, and my locks developed a style of their own. The momentum was like riding in my husband's old red convertible back in the day, speeding with the top down. Finally, I landed. I opened my eyes and blinked several times to enhance my vision. I was standing on a narrow road in a long line of people and I was at the end of the line. Unaware of my location, I stood there frightened and speechless. I turned my head slightly and was immediately awestruck; the place was absolutely breathtaking. The street was pure gold and I could see white clouds in the distance. From where I was standing, they appeared whiter than snow. "Either I'm dreaming, or I'm in paradise," I thought to myself. But I didn't see any houses or buildings; my surroundings were quiet and empty. Where was I? Who were these people?

This couldn't be the town of Simpson, not the town of Simpson, where I had been raised. Because the road was so narrow, we all walked in a single line. Fear propelled me, as we moved forward, with everyone else singing to the soft music that I had just now realized was permeating the atmosphere. Their voices blended perfectly and the melodies were quite gratifying. It was nothing like the choir I had directed for many years. The music continued, but I didn't see any musicians.

For a moment, I tuned out my surroundings and focused on the beautiful singing. Then I quickly snapped back. It troubled me that I couldn't sing along with them, but I had never heard that song before and didn't know the lyrics. Although I had sung many songs from the Baptist hymnal, this had not been one of them.

I could feel the tears welling in my eyes. Everyone was rejoicing but me. By the look on their faces, I assumed my companions were very happy because they seemed to know where they were going and why they were there. Why is everyone rejoicing but me? I thought, with tears welling up in my eyes. My fear began to overtake me and I could feel the hairs rising on my head. If I stood any closer to the person in front of me, he would probably hear the loud pounding of my heart. I didn't want him to turn around because he probably would have thought I was intoxicated, judging by the way my legs were wobbling. I didn't dare extend my hand to introduce myself either because I was shaking like a leaf.

Approximately thirty people formed the line, Black and White men, women, and children. All, except me, were dressed in long white robes, trimmed in gold. I was wearing a plain black robe with no embellishment. I had no idea how my clothes had changed because originally, I had been wearing a blue and white suit. I admired the robes of my companions; they were the most beautiful ones I had ever seen. "But wait a minute!" I mumbled. "If I'm not dressed like them, then I must be in the wrong place. I have to get out of here!" I could not control my tears as I kept asking myself, "What am I going to do?" I turned to locate a possible exit, but the road was too long. It appeared to be endless. I wasn't about to follow it, especially not knowing where it would take me. After standing there pondering for a few moments, I wondered if the man in front of me could help me. In desperation, I reached out and tapped him firmly on the shoulder. "Sir," I whispered, "do you know where we are and where this road will take us?"

He didn't respond. He just kept singing, as if he had not heard me. His behavior startled me even more. Who were these people who could sing, but not communicate? I didn't belong with them. I had to find a way to get out of the line.

I was becoming agitated. It felt as if I had been there for hours and I desperately wanted to find out what was happening. The only thing I remembered was being at an important church meeting earlier that same day. I needed some answers. I didn't want to stand in line any longer, so I stepped out onto the greenest lawn I had ever seen. Looking down, I was reminded of the scripture, "He maketh me to lie down in green pastures...." I had decided to go to the front of the line to try to determine where I was heading.

A demanding voice ordered me back in line. From the direction of the sound, I knew the voice had come from the front. It sounded familiar. Naw. It couldn't be who I thought it was. There was no way he could be here in this place. I tuned the voice out of my mind.

Immediately, I got back on the road and stood there paralyzed with fear. I was too frightened to say anything. Eventually, the line shortened enough that I could see we were approaching an expansive magnificent golden gate. "And he measured the wall thereof, an hundred and forty and four cubits, according to the measure of a man, that is, of the angel" (Revelation 20: 17). On the right were about ten steps leading to a door.

A tall man dressed in the same robe as the others stood near the gate. On his head was a crown sprinkled with diamonds which radiated brilliantly beyond comparison. I was even more captivated by his eyes, which were like flames of fire. I felt my stomach tightening up into knots. I was certain that his was the voice that had ordered me back in line. As individuals arrived at the gate, he checked off their names in a book and directed them to the door on the right. When I got close enough, I could tell that those entering the gate continued singing the song they had sung on the road.

Thank God. It was my turn; relief swept over me. Smiling with reassurance, I walked slowly toward the gate, knowing that my name would be called next. I was finally about to find out why I was here. But the man just lifted his head and stared into my eyes without saying a word. Then he closed the book and walked briskly away to join the others.

I stood there in awe. There was no way was he going to leave me standing here alone. Before he reached the steps,

I yelled to him, "Hey, Mister, I'm supposed to be next." He stopped abruptly and faced me, with that same glare in his eyes. Feeling a resurgence of fear, I continued. "Didn't you see me standing in line? I'm Tina Mae Black. I'm supposed to be next."

"Your name is not in this book," he spoke with authority. His response was cold and matter-of-fact. He showed absolutely no sign that he was in the least concerned about my reaction to being left out.

"What do you mean my name is not in the book?" My fear was being replaced by confusion and a hint of agitation. "What kind of book is that anyway?"

He held up the book so that I could see it clearly. It was gigantic, gold colored, and trimmed with white pearl. "This is the Book of Righteousness and...,"

"The Book of Righteousness?"

Rubbing my forehead as if that would make all of this go away, I tried to digest what he had said. I began pacing back and forth. "Oh no, I can't be in paradise. I must be dreaming."

"If that's the Book of Righteousness," I began pleading, "there's no way my name is not in it. I've had been a Christian just about all my life. This has to be a mistake."

I just stood there pointing in the direction of the book and begging, "Pleassssse, Sir, look again. I go to church every Sunday. And although I don't read my Bible every day, I'm still saved."

Obviously appalled by my statement, he retorted, "This book is NOT about going to church every Sunday. It's about having a pure in heart. The person who went before you was the last name on the list. Your name simply is not here!"

"Then I shouldn't have been in line with the others," I argued. My thoughts were racing a mile a minute. What does he mean by saying my heart is not pure? That must be why the man in front of me didn't communicate. He knew I wasn't like him. What am I going to do now?

His voice brought me back to reality. It was as if he had read my mind.

"You were in line because everyone travels the same road here. But after you reach the Golden Gate, you're separated by the color of your robe."

I kept going over in my head what he had said, that I was the only person wearing a black robe because I didn't have a pure heart, so that's why my name was not in the Book.

"That makes no sense to me," I heard myself blurting out." I'm a Christian, so my name should be there!"

I could tell by the expression on his face that he was outraged. He was obviously not accustomed to someone challenging him that way. He threw up his hands in exasperation.

"Someone else will come to speak with you. My job here is done. I must go now and join the others." He walked swiftly up the steps and just as he was about to disappear through the gate, I knelt down and began to beg again.

"Sir, please don't leave me. You don't understand. I was at a special church meeting. I must go back. They need me there."

The man stared at me for a moment, but didn't speak. A sudden flow of panic overtook me, and tears streamed down my face. Reaching out my hands in desperation, I pleaded, "Could you, could you just show me--- me--- how to get back where I belong? I don't want to be here." I was now speaking in a whisper.

The man began fidgeting. "The others are waiting for me. I must go," he insisted." My job is finished; someone will speak with you." He was rushing to get inside the gate, leaving me standing there, alone.

I didn't know what else to do, so I bowed my head and prayed. My voice trembled, "Lord, please help me. If I can't go with the others, please let me go back. I really don't understand why I'm here."

Out of nowhere, I heard a thundering noise. Was I about to get an answer to my prayer? I never before felt such force. The sensation was like an earthquake and it made my whole body tremble. I stopped praying, stood up quickly, and turned my attention toward the sound, but I didn't dare utter a word. "Why do you want to go back?" the demanding voice inquired, frightening me even more.

I twirled around, trying to determine where the voice was coming from. I didn't see anyone, so I responded to the empty atmosphere. "Who are you? Where are you?" I shouted.

The answer came with an ear piercing resonance, "I'm the one in charge and I'll tell you why you're here!"

CHAPTER TWO

I simply could not fathom not having my name in the Book of Righteousness. It was like a slap in the face. I was Tina Mae Black, well known in Simpson and Gastonia Church. My name should have been listed. I dreaded being the goat separated from the sheep. Don't get me wrong. Paradise was a beautiful place, but I didn't want to be there if I wasn't a sheep.

With my hands clasped as if I were about to pray, I looked in the direction of the thundering Voice. Standing there, I wondered if that Voice was going to let me go back to my special church meeting after he explained why I was here. I couldn't remember whether I had been at the meeting long enough to reveal my secret plan. If not, all my preparation for the last two years had been in vain. I had planned to drop a bomb shell of a secret at that meeting. My family was depending on me to fulfill my father's wish, so I had to get back to finish my task.

The Voice interrupted my thought. Just like before, I heard a loud thundering noise erupting over from the right. “Tina Mae Black,” he said loudly, “Come closer so that I can tell you why you are here.”

Taking small steps, I could see another road to my left. It was not like the road I had traveled. It was a narrow tar covered highway. Being distraught and confused, I chose not to focus on the road. The closer I got to the Golden Gate, the better view I had of my surroundings. I grabbed the front of my robe tightly, breathing rapidly when I saw the word “Hell” printed on a large sign. I stopped abruptly. Surely I was dreaming. Then I thought I heard a male voice screaming. “Please, Sir,” the man pleaded, “I don’t want to go on that road! Please don't make me get on that road!”

My legs felt weak, but my fear propelled me forward. “This is not for real,” I heard myself saying under my breath. “I must be dreaming because Hell is not my home.”

All my life I had gone to church. I was in Sunday school every Sunday and even taught for a year after

Becky had become ill. In addition, I had been choir director for many years. It certainly wasn't my fault that the choir members voted me out. Not a day went by that I had not said my prayers. Not reading my Bible everyday shouldn't have put me in danger of going to Hell either. I was perplexed, so I rubbed my forehead and whispered to myself, "What have I done? What have I done?"

Still trying to rationalize my situation, I thought back over my life and, as crazy as it may sound, couldn't think of any of the Ten Commandments I had disobeyed. I know. I must have been delusional. If the Voice had brought me here to put me on that road to Hell, I would fight because Hell will not be my home.

Before I could speak, I had a flashback to age ten. I had attended a Sunday morning worship service with my best friend Barbara. Her father was the pastor of Tomar Church on the west side of Simpson. We lived right across the road from each other and did everything together. Pastor Gibson was expounding on separating the sheep from the goats and the service seemed never-ending, so Barbara and I were fidgeting. We really wanted to leave, but suddenly, Pastor Gibson stared directly into my eyes, demanding my attention.

"Tina Mae," he shouted as I jumped in my seat like a startled rabbit, "Don't be that goat dressed in a black robe. That will lead you to Hell. You want to be the sheep with a pure heart, dressed in a white robe." He then stood there for a moment, staring at me before continuing his sermon.

Barbara grabbed my hand and squeezed it tightly; she and I both knew by his tone that Pastor Gibson was sincere. I leaned closer to her and whispered, "I'm not going to Hell because Hell is not my home." She chuckled with relief. "Me neither," she whispered back.

That was then, but this was now. Looking down at my black robe, I reflected on what Pastor Gibson had said to me long ago and felt the urge to weep. I had broken that promise. I never understood why he had directed those words to me. Maybe it had been revealed to him in a vision. Anyway, I guess I will never know.

Returning my focus to the Voice, I asked, "Are you sending me on that road over there?" And then I repeated what I said when I was ten years old, "I'm not going to Hell because Hell is not my home."

“I’m in charge here and you will abide by my will,” the Voice replied with authority, echoes reverberating in all directions.

My attitude changed instantly; the Voice was serious. I unfolded my hands and stood at attention like a soldier. I wanted to know what had happened to the man pleading on the other road.

The Voice told me I would find out soon because I would be summoned to join him. “Both of you will share the same fate,” he said unemotionally.

I began sweating profusely. When the tears came and mingled with the sweat, I was unable to see, so I wiped the sweat away with my hands. Then my emotions got the best of me, and I began yelling like a crazy person.

“I don’t belong here! You've got this all wrong! You've got to do something! This just isn't right!”

The Voice's response to my outburst was very calm and matter-of-fact. He instructed me to remain silent until he could review the book of my life, and then he would gladly tell me specifically why I was here. Then I would be on my way down the road to Hell.

I didn't know what my book would reveal or how the Voice would interpret what he saw there, but I did know that I could not think of anything that I felt merited my being on my way to eternal damnation. But suddenly it hit me. Maybe it was my secret plan. That had to be it! The members at Gastonia Church were responsible for my being here. They didn't like me and had caused me to sin. I resolved to fight harder to go back. Those church folks would not prevail! In spite of the obstacles I was facing, I was going to keep the faith and fight to go back to my family.

The Voice walked toward me and allowed me to see the pages of my book. What I saw devastated me. I was lying in a hospital bed connected to numerous monitors. I felt the onslaught of a panic attack. "Why am I in the hospital?" I asked him. "The last thing I remember was being at an important church meeting."

"Let me refresh your memory," the Voice began. "You were at the special church meeting trying to hinder the decisions of the Official Board. While you were revealing your secret plan, you experienced dizziness. You became disoriented and passed out. When the paramedics arrived, you were transported to the hospital."

I began to put the puzzle together. I had passed out and they took me to the hospital. My spirit had left my body and come here, a place I did not want to be.

As I continued reviewing my Book of Life, I saw Dr. Ellis and the nurse standing over me, rechecking my vital signs. Their expressions revealed that things did not look good. Dr. Ellis had been unsuccessful in finding the medication that would lower my blood pressure quickly. He was worried, and watching him by way of an out-of-body experience, I was beside myself.

I looked away, trying to hold back tears. When I could bring myself to continue viewing, I saw my husband enter the room and sit beside my bed. He stared at me lovingly and held my hand. I was overcome with grief at the thought of not seeing him again. "I will not leave my husband," I heard myself saying. "I'm not going on that road because Hell is not my home!"

I wanted to console him, but of course, I could not; I felt helpless. His countenance was so sad, but there was nothing I could do. I couldn't even tell him that my spirit had left my body.

My husband and I had met twenty five years ago at Gastonia Church. I remembered the night he had introduced himself to me at one of my choir rehearsals. He still had on his chef's uniform that smelled like the foods he had prepared during that day. He had come directly to church from work, without taking time to go home to shower and change. But that didn't matter. His handsome face, his tall, slim physique and his big brown eyes, mesmerized me.

I used to tease him about how loudly he sang. I could hear his voice over everyone in the choir and, as is often, the case with those who sing the loudest, he could not carry a tune in a bucket.

"Jerome can't sing a lick!" my mom used to tease. Be that as it may, he sang in the choir for four years before God touched the heart of the pastor to make him a deacon. Oh Happy Day!

Suddenly, a thought entered my mind. I wondered if the horrible secret I had withheld from Jerome was in my Book of Life. You see, Jerome and I had been planning to renew our vows in several months. But if I had to reveal what I've done, I'm sure there would be no renewal, not this year anyway. But then "reality" sank in; why was I concerned about that. If I was not allowed to go back, that was a moot point.

My heart sank when I saw my daughter Lisa enter the room. Wiping tears from my eyes, I was unable to restrain my emotions. We had not spoken in two years. On her last visit, she had become furious when I asked her to be a part of my family's secret plan. "I simply won't do it, mother," she interrupted, talking over me. "Those members are going to be outraged when you reveal what you've done. I won't be a part of it." Then she stormed out of the house, threatening never to return.

Lisa was born one year after I got married. It was the happiest day of our lives, and Jerome adored his little girl. As she grew up, everyone used to say that she looked just like him, although she was my height.

Lisa was residing in Atlanta, Georgia, so she had driven three hours to get to the hospital. "My daughter is visiting me because my condition is serious," I said to the Voice. "I can't leave her like this. Please let me go back!"

The Voice did not respond. I felt a lump in my throat. I stood there watching my daughter, wanting to reach out to reassure her and tell her how sorry I was for not listening to her. Maybe if I had listened, I wouldn't be in this predicament. But with Lisa being there, it showed that she had forgiven me. I just had to go back to make things right.

I then took my focus off Lisa and my husband and concentrated on what was happening at the hospital. It was a matter of life or death. If I wanted to be with them again, I had to fight to go back.

Dr. Ellis told Lisa and my husband that there was nothing else he could do. My condition remained grave. Lisa wept silently while her father tried to console her. I missed them terribly and wished that I could call out to them and explain what was happening to me. I was not inside the body in that hospital room. I was pleading for my life in a place I did not want to be---HELL.

Then I heard Dr. Ellis whisper to the nurse, "I've never had a patient remain unconscious for this length of time and survive. We'd better monitor her non-stop. If she doesn't come around by midnight, I'll call in a specialist." I glanced down at my arm to see what time it was and realized that I was no longer wearing my watch. As a matter of fact, I was not wearing any of the jewelry I had adorned myself with before heading to my church meeting. But that was irrelevant at the moment. "What's going to happen to me if I don't recover by midnight?" I asked the Voice. "And how many more hours do I have to wait?"

"You have several hours before midnight," he said.

"And then what's going to happen?" I asked again, feeling my anxiety heighten.

"You'll review that in your book of life," he told me calmly.

"But I want to know now! Just tell me whether I'm going back or down that road. Just get it over with!"

If I didn't regain consciousness, I knew I would be headed down that road to Hell, never again to see my family. I could not bear the thought.

The Voice answered with more force, "You will abide by my will! Continue viewing your Book of Life."

Reluctantly, I continued my reviewing. Seeing Jerome sitting there with his head bowed in prayer was more than I could take. Lisa looked exhausted. She had stopped crying, but her eyes were red and puffy. The two of them joined hands and continued in prayer.

"Will their prayer requests be granted?" I asked the Voice. "This experience has been so traumatic for them."

The Voice did not answer right away. I could not believe how stoic he was considering the circumstances. I threw back my shoulders with wounded pride and exhaled an indignant sigh. "Will their prayers be answered?" I asked again. "Will you allow me to go back?" I had asked that question so much that I was beginning to sound like a broken record.

The Voice expressed no empathy. "That will be reviewed in your Book of Life."

I was agitated. I wanted a verbal response. Why couldn't the Voice just answer my questions? The thought of not going back to my family was too painful. I did not want to see them suffering this way. Losing my parents had been painful enough, but the pain of losing my husband and my daughter would be like nothing I had ever experienced.

Just standing there, I contemplated my options and realized that they were nonexistent. Being controlled by someone else was a challenge. I was usually the aggressor and told other people what to do, and they would do it. The tides had turned, and I didn't like it one little bit. Knowing I could not leave when I wanted to was like being in a prison of sorts. I began wishing I had done some things differently. But I still maintained that I had been too good a person to be in my current predicament.

I tried harder to remember what I might have done to endanger me of the fires of Hell. But my thoughts were clouded. In my mind, there was nothing I had done so horrific would land me in a place I didn't wanted to be. I had no other choice but to keep fighting to go back.

I remembered reading the scripture, "For all have sinned, and come short of the glory of God". . . Huh? We all have shortcomings? I didn't want my mind to go there. I thought I had been living a relatively sin-free existence. I thought I had been doing it right, but maybe not.

I decided that if I kept pestering the Voice, maybe sooner or later he would stop requiring me to look into my Book of Life and just tell me my fate. But I was wrong. His response came in such a thundering sound that it almost took my breath away. And this time, I could tell he was really impatient.

"EVERYTHING YOU WANT TO KNOW WILL BE REVEALED IN YOUR BOOK OF LIFE! CONTINUE REVIEWING!"

His directive seemed final, but I continued muttering to myself. I didn't dare speak loudly enough for him to hear me.

"Why can't he just let me go back? I'm not giving up this fight. Reviewing my Book of Life is torture and serves only to prolong my stay here. All I want to know is why? If I could just remember what happened at the special church meeting before I had the dizzy spell, I would know why I am here."

CHAPTER THREE

There is nothing like the aroma of a sweet cup of coffee to start my day. This was especially true on Friday, May 9, 2014, as I sat at my kitchen table, sipping my morning cup and rejoicing. Finally, I was going to reveal my family secret plan at the special church meeting. I had promised my father that I would keep the legacy of the McMann family at Gastonia Church intact. Unfortunately, that legacy had been taken away two years ago. But at that special meeting tonight, the McMann family would regain control.

My father, Rev. Billy McMann, Sr., had pastored Gastonia Church for forty years. Three years ago, he had suffered a massive heart attack while preaching the Sunday morning message. He was now resting in the arms of Jesus. I remember very vividly wiping away my tears at my father's funeral and vowing never to let him down. I would make sure that his dying wishes were carried out.

My father was tall and hefty gentleman, who at age 80 didn't look a day over 60. He was proud that his dark brown skin had fewer wrinkles than most people his age. His life was Gastonia Church, and he ignored the members who often complained that the church had become his obsession. After all, it was a family church founded by his father's descendants in 1865.

Of course, my mother disagreed with my father's idea of pastoring, which was using intimidation to coerce the members to give money, even beyond the tithe. If my mother had been alive, no way would she have participated in his plan to keep the McManns in control of Gastonia Church. She never supported him on anything he did for the church, anyway. My mother had passed away four years before my father. Oftentimes, he had told me how much I resembled her. She was a beautiful lady, petite, fair skinned, with shoulder length black wavy hair that she wore in a bun.

But as far as our personalities, there was no resemblance, well maybe except for my aggressiveness. My mother mostly kept to herself; she was an introvert. I remember vividly the day she revealed to us that she was been diagnosed with stomach cancer. It shocked the family, of course. In spite of her illness, she tried to keep the family from grieving. My mother was high-spirited until the day she died.

But my father had been my rock. I loved him and would do anything for him. After all, I was his favorite out of all of his children. I just know he would have been pleased with my secret plan to keep the legacy of the McMann family intact. I was the only one in the family he could depend on, and I felt obliged to fulfill his request, God rest his soul.

My husband walked into the kitchen and lightly kissed me on the lips. "You're in a good mood," Jerome said, joining me at the kitchen table with his cup of coffee. "You were singing so loudly coming downstairs that I'm sure everyone in Simpson heard you. I haven't heard you sing like that since you were voted as choir director," he joked.

"Good mood? Of course," I replied smiling back at him. I sat back in my chair placing my large cup of coffee on the table. "I'm ecstatic, honey."

Jerome stopped sipping his coffee and looked at me. His eyes twinkled, but his grin faded when he realized I was serious. "You know why I'm ecstatic?" "Huh." "Pastor Arnold Knighton will get what's coming to him. Two years of waiting have been long enough. I'll never forgive him for what he's done to the McMann family. My father's ancestors built Gastonia Church in 1865, and he took away our legacy. Because of him, no member of the McMann family holds a position in the church. Pastor Knighton's days are numbered. I won't let my father down. I'll keep my promise to him."

"Tina, are you sure you're going to pull this off?" he asked, with skepticism.

"You mean my secret plan? Of course I will Jerome. If all my contacts are at that special meeting tonight, I have nothing to worry about. They promised me that they would support me. Based on what I told them about Rev. Knighton, they'll keep their word."

I hadn't told my husband or anyone the full extent of my plan. If they knew, they would have not agreed to participate. I wanted my husband to believe in me. I took his hand and spoke softly, "Don't worry, Jerome; I know what I'm doing. Everything will be just fine. I can't wait to see the expression on the members' faces, especially Rev. Knighton. It's not that I don't like him. I just won't forgive him for what he's done to our family."

Once I said that, I realized how ridiculous it must have sounded to my husband. He stared at me with uncertainty in his eyes. He wasn't convinced, so I continued to speak.

"You know, I blame Deacon Michael Brown for recommending Rev. Knighton to become our pastor. He really didn't tell the members too much about him before he was elected. The McMann family didn't vote for him anyway. His background was too sketchy and he was too private."

All we knew about Rev. Knighton was that he was in his early thirties. He was unmarried, had no transportation, and resided at a hotel. Those things upset me. He was elected as the youngest pastor of Gastonia Church ever. I also blamed the Deacon Board for going along with Deacon Brown's recommendation, which was obviously biased because he and Rev. Knighton were very close.

"Tina, I think you need to re-think what you're up against," Jerome pressed, concerned that I was digging a hole for myself.

The doorbell interrupted our conversation. I looked at the clock on the stove and wondered who on earth would be visiting us as early as 8:05 a.m. Certain the caller was there to see me, Jerome headed into the den to check the newspaper to see if our special meeting had been advertised as I had requested.

I went into the foyer, disarmed the alarm, and then I walked to the door. "Who is it?" I yelled through the closed door.

"It's me Tina," I heard a familiar voice call out.

I chuckled. "Donald, is that you?"

"Yea, it's me," he responded. "Hurry and open the door!"

As soon as I opened it Donald brushed past me as though he were being chased. From his action, I thought he was late for work since he was dressed in his blue uniform. He was the custodian at Simpson Elementary School, where I had taught for 30 years.

"Are you on your way to work?"

"No," he said, looking around the room with his eyes widening.

"Where's Jerome? I want to talk to the both of you right away."

Donald appeared frightened. In fact, he looked like he had seen a ghost.

"Are you ok? Would you like a cup of coffee?"

"No Tina."

I directed Donald into the den, where he sat down on the sofa, his hands shaking nervously. Donald and his family had lived next door for many years. He was my husband's first cousin and the brother he never had. They even had similar features, but my husband was about two inches taller. They both had brown eyes and mesmerizing physiques. Jerome was 55 years old and Donald was 50, but their age difference had never interfered with their friendship.

Donald's life had not been without its share of ups and downs. His wife suffered with severe depression and anxiety after discovering his infidelity. His actions had traumatized their three children, Cameron aged 10, Janie aged 15, and John aged 17. John and Janie had been students in my math class at Simpson Elementary School.

It was John, the oldest, who had tried to keep the family intact. He had come over to visit one day and expressed his concerned about his father.

"Please encourage him to come back to church," he pleaded. "I hate seeing him like this. I don't want my dad to be a backslider!"

After my father passed away, Donald had been dismissed from the Deacon Board for cheating on his wife with one of the choir members, whom he had gotten pregnant. Selfishly, I had enticed him to return to church and assist with our secret plan. After all, our situations were similar. We both had been dismissed from our positions and unwillingly accepted our fates.

Jerome finally spoke, "Good morning, cuz. What brings you by so early this morning?"

"Good morning Jerome. Sorry to bother you, but I really need to discuss our secret plan."

When I heard him say our secret plan, I sat down in my matching love seat.

"You said our secret plan?" I repeated." What are you talking about, Donald?"

After two years of planning, I didn't want anything to go wrong. Donald looked at me and then back at Jerome.

"I don't know how to explain what happened last night, but it made me very uncomfortable. I –ah – I ah"

"Donald, please! Just tell us what happened," begged my husband.

Donald sighed and glanced over at me. I could see the pleading in his eyes as he continued. "Tina, don't go through with your secret plan. Something terrible might happen to you."

"What are you talking about, Donald?"

"Well, I ah- I ah," he began stuttering again.

Why didn't he just get on with it? We didn't have all day.

Donald murmured something about having had a bad dream last night.

"I woke up in the middle of the night, frantic," he said. "I tossed and turned until day break. I just know it was a warning to withdraw our secret plan."

Then he looked back at Jerome, as if waiting for an answer of agreement to stop me.

Donald was making no sense. Anyone could have a dream. Maybe it was something he had eaten.

"Donald just had a nightmare," I reassured him.

"It wasn't a nightmare, Tina. You don't understand! It was a warning! You were at the church meeting revealing your secret plan. Suddenly, you were attacked. I couldn't see what it was. Something abruptly took you out of the church. You were screaming for help, but no one could protect you."

I looked at my husband, at first puzzled, and then I started to laugh. Donald was over-reacting. I was not in the least intimidated by his warning. I had everything under control. I told Donald not to worry, that everything would be fine if we followed through with our plan, but he seemed annoyed.

"The two of you might not believe me, but I'm sure someone will," he said, indicating that he would reveal the plan to someone else.

Now dead serious, I asked, "Donald, have you told anybody what we're planning tonight?"

"Don't worry, Tina," he said. "Our secret is safe with me. After all, I'm part of it now. But my dream made me realize that I am being a hypocrite. That's why I wish you would reconsider. I've already asked for forgiveness because I don't want to hurt those church people."

I didn't understand how Donald's nightmare had anything to do with our secret plan. It all seemed absurd to me. I didn't want him to renege on our plan. After all, the meeting was tonight. I couldn't get a replacement on such short notice.

Jerome began pleading with Donald.

"Come on, man! We need your assistance. Who will I get to work with me at this late date? You know I can't trust just anyone."

I wanted to tell Donald to get out of my house right then and there.

"Don't you guys depend on me for anything? I've made my decision."

"Man - don't point your finger at me," Jerome said. Donald continued, "Neither my wife nor I will be at that meeting tonight. You can bank on that. And I have prayed that you two will see the light. My conscious won't let me be a part of anything unrighteous. I know it was a warning, Tina. I've never had a dream like that before. I shouldn't have let you talk me into helping you in the first place."

I got up and walked toward the kitchen door. I wanted him to leave. I stood there for a moment staring at him.

"Okay Donald, I've heard quite enough," I told him. "You've ruined our plan! End of discussion! I can't believe you have betrayed us in this way!"

Donald seemed disheartened and about to cry as he took a few steps toward the door.

"No Tina," he said, pointing upward, "I haven't ruined your plan; you've ruined HIS plan!"

The clock on the stove read 8:23 a.m. I had almost forgotten my 9:30 a.m. doctor's appointment. Thank God, I had a welcomed distraction. I had heard just about enough of Donald's nonsense. I had gone to the doctor the week before for my physical and was told that I had borderline hypertension. I had gained ten pounds and Dr. Ellis was concerned. He had told me to return for another reading on Friday, May 9, 2014. As I headed upstairs to get ready, I looked at Jerome, hoping he would be able to pick up my telepathic message to try to convince Donald to go along with our plan. Instead, Jerome asked if I wanted him to accompany me to my doctor's appointment.

"No, I'll be fine," I reassured. "I have to go, I'm already running late."

"Tina, please wait." Donald tried to defend himself. He knew I was still upset. His tone was sad.

"How can you get your reward humiliating Rev. Knighton and the members? You know they're going to be outraged. And laughing at me about the dream, you shouldn't have. It was a warning."

I ignored him and continue upstairs. Walking toward the closet to get an outfit, I suddenly felt dizzy and disoriented. My head was spinning out of control. I had never experienced that before, so I held onto the closet door. When I felt slightly better, I walked the few steps to my bed and sat down.

After I sat there for what seemed like about ten minutes, the dizziness subsided. I pondered what to do. I decided that it wouldn't be a good idea to tell my husband because that would have been the end of my plan to attend the church meeting that evening. I just chalked my episode up to my being anxious about what I was planning to accomplish at the church meeting. And Donald's "warning" certainly had not helped. Yes, that had to be it.

Time was of the essence. I didn't want to miss my appointment. It was important to me to get my blood pressure checked. I took off my robe and was ready to slip on my blue and white pant suit when I had a change of heart. I would wear that to the meeting this evening. Instead, I threw on a pair of jeans and a white tee-shirt.

THE VOICE

"Review your Book of Life," I heard the Voice demand again. When I looked again, I saw Donald sitting in our living room, pleading with us to abandon the plan. Maybe he had been right all along. He said that "something" had taken me away from the church, and no one had been able to help me. But if I was here because of our secret plan, then Donald should be here too. After all, he had had an affair; he was certainly no saint.

I cried out to the Voice, "I don't want to travel that road alone! Please let me go back! Am I here because I enticed Donald to go astray?"

The Voice repeated, "I'm in control. You will abide by my will. Continue reviewing your Book of Life."

CHAPTER FOUR

Friday morning Deacon Michael Brown arrived at Gastonia Church at 9:05 a.m. to meet with Rev. Knighton. He was overwhelmed with joy. All the remodeling and special projects entrusted to his supervision had been completed. His only concern at that moment was Tina Mae's reaction. At the special church meeting two years ago, she had blurted out, "This church doesn't need any remodeling. That's too much money." Tina Mae had made such a scene that one of the deacons had escorted her out of the sanctuary.

Deacon Brown chuckled when he remembered that Tina Mae had never objected to any renovation projects that her father had proposed to the membership. At that same meeting, Tina Mae had lashed out at Rev. Knighton for removing her husband from his position as Chairman of the Deacon Board. The new Chairman was elected by a majority vote, but she was angry with Rev. Knighton nonetheless. The new chairman was trustworthy, unlike Tina Mae's husband, so Rev. Knighton chose just to ignore her meddling.

Tina Mae was also harboring resentment toward Rev. Knighton because she believed he had made his niece Carrie church secretary, replacing her sister Rebecca. She had failed to realize, however, that the members were fed up with her sister's snippy attitude toward them and had voted Rebecca out of that position.

Carrie didn't see Deacon Brown when he entered her office because she was so focused on her computer screen.

"Good morning, Uncle Mike," she said after hearing him speak. "You startled me. I didn't even see you standing there."

Carrie could not conceal her look of surprise when she saw Deacon Brown dressed in his "Sunday-go-to-meeting" attire. The gray suit was complementing his dark complexion. To set it off, he wore a black striped tie and matching handkerchief. Glancing at the antique clock on the wall, he announced, "I have a 9:30 appointment with Rev. Knighton."

Carrie reached for the phone on the black credenza desk and buzzed Rev. Knighton to let him know that Deacon Brown had arrived. As he waited, he sat in a chair across from Carrie's desk, surveying the room and marveling at how beautiful it looked now that the remodeling was complete.

The beige carpet had been replaced, and where the old Apple computer once rested now sat a new sleek HP that was sure to have all the features that would make Carrie's job seemingly effortless. The walls had been freshly painted and were decorated with sconces and pictures of bible scenes. It didn't even look like the same office.

Since he was early for his appointment, he decided to leave and come back at the exact time. Actually, Deacon Brown wanted to be alone. He disappeared inside the sanctuary and sat down on one of pews. With his head bowed and eyes staring at the beautiful green carpet, he reflected on his life back in the day. He recalled the first time he had visited the original Gastonia Church. His mother had brought him there to visit when he was only six years old. Ten years later, he became a member.

He worked diligently and showed himself to be a true servant of the people, so much so that within a short time, he was ordained as a Deacon. And two years ago, he had been named chairman of the Deacon Board, replacing Deacon Black. He had vivid memories of the old church, which had been located a distance from the main highway in a wooded area lined with trees on both sides of the road. For miles, there were no buildings or houses. At night it was pitch dark and eerie. A chill ran through his body upon reflection. He remembered feeling glad about joining the new church. He knew that when he turned sixteen and got his license, his mother would expect him to drive her down the dark, creepy highway to prayer meeting every Wednesday night, and he certainly was not looking forward to that. The thought made him chuckle out loud.

Suddenly his smile faded, and tears welled in his eyes. Deacon Brown wished his mother were alive to see how Gastonia Church had been transformed. She had passed away suddenly on her way to work one morning five years ago. A drunk driver hit her head on, killing her instantly. The Deacon rested his head against the pew, wiping the tears rolling down his face. He thanked God that although his mother was no longer with him, at least her prayer had been answered. Tina Mae Black had finally been dismissed as choir director because of her inappropriate behavior.

"Hallelujah!" he shouted.

Deacon Brown had been super excited when the members were forced to relocate Gastonia Church to Simpson. Condominiums were to be built on the old property, but the members didn't mind the move in the least. The old church was in dire need of repairs. The floors creaked. There was only one unisex bathroom and you could always count on having to wait in a long line. Moving the church to Simpson was a huge blessing!

Deacon Brown looked down at his watch. He still had a few more minutes before his meeting with Rev. Knighton. Sitting there thinking, he was glad that Rev. Knighton was no way the kind of pastor that Rev. McMann had been. After the church was relocated, Rev. McMann had given his family members positions of leadership. It is never a good idea for a church to be family run.

The members were not pleased, but they had accepted their pastor's decision because they felt intimidated by him. Rev. McMann was aging, and his of ability to expound on the word had been steadily deteriorating. Hardly anyone attended services, and the membership had declined from 500 to 75 members.

Deacon Brown rose out of his seat and walked near the pulpit. Standing there, he recalled the Sunday Rev. McMann passed away. The choir had just finished singing a spiritual.

Rev. McMann had stood to approach the podium when he paused suddenly, grabbing his chest, and began gasping for breath. Before anyone realized what was happening, he fell. Fear spread over the congregation. Deacon Brown, who was a nurse by profession, rushed to the pulpit, calling Rev. McMann's name. When he did not respond, Deacon Brown administered CPR, but to no avail.

When the paramedics arrived, he was pronounced dead. He had suffered a massive heart attack. Because of his obsession with Gastonia Church, Rev. McMann had not abided by the doctor's order. He should have retired several years earlier.

Deacon Brown had been made Deacon under Rev. McMann's leadership, so he was disappointed when it was revealed that Rev. McMann had some deep dark secrets and was not the pastor he had professed to be.

When he was twelve years old his father divorced his mother. He looked up to Rev. McMann as a father figure and wanted him to be his role model. But instead he was arrogant and self-centered. The members were brainwashed by his intimidation. Every Sunday at worship service, he stood behind the podium wearing two faces. Dressed in his black robe trimmed in red uttering his famous word, "You talked the talked, but you don't walk the walk. He didn't practice what you preached.

Deacon Brown was disturbed when he had discovered Rev. McMann had embezzled $100,000 from the church. The finances were almost depleted. He had appointed his sister, Minnie Blackwell, as finance secretary so he could control the book.

Deacon Brown was grateful that she explained to the Deacon Board about the missing money after he was deceased. Everyone was petrified by him and his family ruling the church. That's why at the last special church meeting, the McMann family was voted out of their positions. Tina Mae Black worshipped the ground he walked on. She thought you could do no wrong.

Deacon Brown's head dropped slightly. Holding back tears, he thought how Rev. McMann had steered the church into bankruptcy. Because of Rev. Knighton's persuasion, the creditors had not closed the church doors.

A chill escaped his body. It was like Rev. McMann had actually been there with him. Deacon Brown was so deep in his thought he had lost track of time. He rushed out of the sanctuary through the double doors and headed swiftly toward Rev. Knighton's office and gently knocked on door before entering. Rev. Knighton was sitting at his brown traditional desk. "Sorry to keep you waiting, Pastor," he apologized.

Rev. Knighton stood up and extended his hand, accepting his apology. Deacon Brown took a seat, reached into his brief case, took out the check off list, and handed it to Rev. Knighton. Glancing at the list, Rev. Knighton said jokingly,

"I assumed everything has been completed to your satisfaction."

Trying to compose himself, he nodded, forcing a smile. Rev. Knighton carefully reviewed the check off list.

"A job well done," he said. "I appreciate your getting everything completed before the meeting tonight." Rev. Knighton's facial expression becoming serious, he folded his arms against his chest matter-of-factly and said,

"Now let's discuss the real reason why I asked you to stop by this morning."

"This meeting is not about what you assigned me to do?"

"Yes. No. Well, it's about something far more important," Rev. Knighton said, clearing his throat.

"Oh, I know. It's about Tina Mae Black and those rumors she been spreading," Deacon Brown replied, leaning forward as if to whisper. "Everyone at Gastonia Church was talking about it after last Sunday's worship service."

Abruptly, Rev. Knighton unfolded his arms and placed his right hand under his chin making eye contact.

"That Tina Mae has been a piece of work since day one. Those rumors will be discussed later. I have more important things to deal with."

For the moment, Deacon Brown allowed himself to get lost in his thoughts. How could Rev. Knighton dismiss those rumors Tina Mae had spread? She had told all of her contacts that the two of them were "gay" and she would be sure to bring it up at the meeting tonight. Snapping out of his thoughts, Deacon Brown straightened himself in his seat and spoke with conviction, "Rev. Knighton, despite Tina Mae's accusation about us and her criticizing the work you have done here at the church, don't be discouraged. Most of the members were relieved when you replaced her father. Without your proficiency, the doors would have been closed."

Rev. Knighton's face lit up. Deacon Brown could tell that the pastor was relieved to know that someone actually appreciated his efforts, so he continued.

"I prayed night and day for a man like you, and God answered my prayers."

Rev. Knighton was well aware of the turmoil that Tina Mae's father had caused in the church, and he had made it his focus to establish an atmosphere of peace and reverence, despite the obvious rebellion of a few. Pushing back his black leather chair, he unlocked a desk drawer and retrieved a long white envelope. Then he handed it to Deacon Brown.

"Please - take this," he said. "It's your Ministerial License. I've signed it. I want you to call the deacons and schedule a meeting for 6:00 p.m. The time has come that we must reveal our secret. Two years has been long enough. The deacons should know what I plan to do."

Deacon Brown hesitated, but Rev. Knighton insisted that he take the envelope. "Please - take it," he repeated. "The deacons must know that you've completed your course to become a minister. And before the election tonight, I plan to ordain you. Rev. Darnell Neil has already agreed to assist me."

For a moment, Deacon Brown sat there speechless. Rev. Neil resided in the same hotel as Rev. Knighton. As a matter of fact, that's where he had met the two of them. One day while he was there having lunch, they had come and joined him. Rev. Knighton and Deacon Brown became close friends.

Deacon Brown was shaking his head in disagreement. "Are you-you sure you want to explain our secret tonight? The members are going to be 'thrown for a loop.' Why tonight?"

"It must be done tonight."

"But why are you insisting it be done tonight? Is it because of Tina Mae?"

"I can't tell you. At the special church meeting tonight, you'll understand why. I'm sorry our secret couldn't be revealed sooner, but Tina Mae would have been trouble for the both of us? You remember what happened when her brother completed his theologian classes. After he was ordained, she begged me to appoint him to be the assistant pastor."

Oh no, he's going to appoint me. I'm not ready to be the assistant pastor. That's why the position has not been filled.

Rev. Knighton paused and changed the subject.

"Tina Mae's husband is a member of the Deacon Board and..."

"And her husband will be attending the Deacons' meeting this evening," Deacon Brown finished his thought.

"I'm sure he's going to tell to her I received my Minister's License. I just know she will cause trouble at the meeting tonight."

Rev. Knighton chuckled and stroked his chin.

"Don't you worry about Tina Mae Black," he said. "I'll handle her! That's why the meeting is set for 6:00 p.m. When you adjourn, it will be time for the special church meeting. He won't have time to tell her. You've completed your classes and there's no point in waiting. There's not a thing she can do about it! I have everything under control!"

No sooner had Rev. Knighton spoken those words, his secretary buzzed to tell him that Tina Mae was on the other line requesting the agenda for tonight's meeting. His curt response,

"Tina Mae- there will be no agenda!" And he hung up, not allowing his secretary time to respond. Then he looked knowingly at Deacon Brown.

"I know why she wants it," he said, but she's not going to run this show!"

The both sat in silence for a brief second and then Rev. Knighton stood, indicating that their meeting had ended and said, "Michael, you're the Deacon I trusted most. It has been a pleasure working with you these past two years. I've always been able to depend on you, but after tonight, there will be some changes. Whatever happens, don't be dismayed; I will stand behind you all the way."

As Deacon Michael Brown stood to leave, Rev. Knighton reached across his desk, extending his hand. "You can count on me," he said with assurance. "I'll see you at the Deacons' meeting."

Deacon Brown walked out of the office, still uncomfortable with what had transpired. This whole thing weighed heavily on his mind. Why does he want to reveal our secret the night of the special church meeting? If he is going to appoint me as the assistant pastor, why didn't he just tell me? Lord, I pray that everything goes well.

* * * * *

Rev. Knighton buzzed Carrie. "For the next hour, I won't be available," he said. "I'll be in the sanctuary, so keep the outside doors locked and take messages for me." Carrie paused.

Reading her thoughts, he continued in a troubled his voice, "I've got something important I need to do before the meeting tonight."

And with that limited explanation, Rev. Knighton walked down the hall into the sanctuary. Intrigued and curious, Carrie tip-toed towards the door and peeped her head inside. Rev. Knighton was at the altar on his knees. She saw him look upward and heard him whisper, "For your sake Tina Mae Black, I hope this prayer will be answered."

CHAPTER FIVE

When I arrived at the doctor's office, the clock on the wall said 9:46 a.m. Because of the dizzy spell I had had earlier, I was fourteen minutes late. But when I looked around the waiting area, I realized that being late was not going to be a problem. It appeared that everyone in Simpson was there waiting to be seen by the doctor.

Anxiety set in because I knew I would have to be there longer than I had expected. I had things to do and places to go. The burden of carrying out my father's wishes weighed heavily on me, but my siblings and contacts were depending on me. I had to follow through.

I picked up a magazine and thumbed through the pages. I was too nervous and impatient to actually read. There was no way I'd be able to concentrate. Before long, I just gave up and placed the magazine back on the coffee table in front of me. Still fidgeting, I turned to the right and looked out the window. It was a beautiful spring day. The blue sky with sparse white puffy clouds took my breath away. I was grateful it had stopped raining before Friday night. The weatherman had predicted inclement weather all week. If the bad weather had continued, I know my contacts would not have attended the special church meeting.

"Good morning Tina Mae!"

Turning around in my seat, I came face to face with Catherine Jenkins. She had taken the seat right next to me.

"Good morning," I said, "glad to have someone to pass the time with."

Catherine, who was in her early fifties, had that chocolate brown complexion and a medium build. She was married to Rev. Ralph Jenkins, an associate minister at Gastonia Church and they were very close friends with Jerome and I. Catherine was a member and lead singer of the Senior Choir. I remember thinking when I was the director, "No one at Gastonia Church sings as well as Catherine." She had that anointed voice that would bring everyone to their feet rejoicing. Last Sunday morning at worship service, she had really blessed me with her rendition of "Amazing Grace."

Although some of the choir members felt that I had showed favoritism to Catherine, I disagreed. Their accusations stemmed from jealousy. Time after time, I had explained to the choir that serious, dedicated choir members do not show malice, jealousy, or envy toward each other. But they sing to uplift Jesus. After I was voted out of my position, Thomas Edward replaced me as the choir director. Unlike me, he refused to allow Catherine to exercise her gift, so she joined the Mass Choir, which only sang at special functions.

"Oh I just arrived," Catherine said with a smile. "What a surprise to see you here at the doctor office. When you blew your car horn at me on Delmar Street, I thought you were on your way someplace else."

I had to bite my tongue to keep from saying, "I blew my horn because you were driving so slow, you made me miss the light." Everyone in Simpson talked about Catherine's lack of driving skills. One would think that she was part of a funeral procession.

"Ms. Tina, when that light changed, you sped off as though you were going to put out a fire," Catherine joked. I chuckled and revealed that I was speeding because I was late for my doctor's appointment.

Catherine then changed the subject. She leaned closer and whispered, “Miss Tina Mae, I was going to call you. I need to apologize about the special church meeting tonight.”

“Apologize? Why?”

Catherine surveyed the room, making sure that no one was listening to our conversation. Whispering even softer, she continued. “I don’t think I will be able to attend.”

It was like a slap in the face. I didn’t see that coming, especially from her. What excuse does she have? I hope she didn’t have a dream like Donald Johnson.

“Is everything okay?” I asked calmly. She nodded. “Then what’s the problem?”

As if on cue, Catherine sneezed. “I’ve been sick all week from all that rain,” she said, trying to sound hoarse. “I think I've caught the flu.” Then she let out a deep cough that resounded in the waiting area.

She was obviously sick, but I felt that something else was going on. She had pressed her way to the doctor, hadn't she? So why couldn't she press her way to the meeting. I was depending on her support. Catherine and Rev. Johnson were a part of my secret plan.

"What about your husband? Will he be at the meeting tonight?

"My- my - husband," Catherine sneezed again. Wiping her nose with a tissue, she changed the subject. "Ms. Tina Mae I – I - have to wait to see what the doctor tells me."

She had left me no choice; I needed plan B right away. Donald's reneging and now Catherine's withdrawals were surprising disappointments. Without their support, what were we going to do on such short notice? I couldn't replace them just like that.

I wanted reassurance. Looking into Catherine's puffy eyes, I asked, "Will you be attending the meeting if you are feeling better by tonight?"

"Yes. Well, I think so," Catherine managed to get out through her coughs and sneezes.

"Please try, Catherine," I pleaded. "And if you can't attend, I hope I can count on Rev. Jenkins for support. For the past two years, he's been promising to support the ministerial ministry."

Catherine was extremely nervous when I mentioned Rev. Jenkins. Her voice trembled. "I know Tina. My – my husband and – and I have supported you faithfully for two years. But- but - you have to understand."

"Understand what?" I asked, getting agitated. "What are you trying to say?"

"Tina Mae Black," the nurse called loudly.

I couldn't believe what I was hearing and I was not about to follow the nurse without finishing this conversation.

"Are you saying that you've been having second thoughts about our secret plan?"

Catherine reached into her purse for another tissue. "Yes, I ah, I've been having second thoughts. I don't know if I can do what you..."

"Tina Mae Black," the nurse repeated.

Catherine just sat there trying to explain, but the words were struck in her throat. The nurse was still waiting for me. I was boiling hot. How dare her tell me she wanted to withdraw on the day of the special church meeting.

Standing up and grabbing my purse, I mumbled "I have to go. Please call me! We'll continue this conversation on the phone."

I walked to the examination room with Catherine's words ringing in my ears. She was obviously nervous about our secret plan. I remembered that she had been hesitant when I first presented it to her, but I thought I had successfully dispelled her fear. "I'll just speak to her later," I thought to myself. I have to focus on Tina Mae right now.

The nurse interrupted my thought. "How are you feeling today, Mrs. Black?"

"Good," I lied. If only you really knew how I'm feeling! I'm having a terrible day! Everything is falling apart!

As I sat on the exam table in the tiny room, staring at white walls, I became more and more furious. I kept telling myself that I had to maintain my composure before the nurse took my readings. If my blood pressure reflected the stress I was actually feeling at the moment, it would be sky high. She flashed a professional smile and told me to stretch out my left arm. When she was done, I watched her beautiful smile suddenly fade. She didn't have to tell me. I knew my numbers were high. Then she confirmed that my blood pressure exceeded what it had been just a week earlier, 160/95. I was a little frightened.

My blood pressure had never been a major problem. I knew it had to be the stress. Dealing with my secret plan for two years had been taxing indeed.

"Dr. Ellis will be in shortly," the nurse said. Then she walked out of the room.

While waiting for Dr. Ellis, I remembered the dizzy spell I had experienced earlier that morning. I was certainly not going to say anything to Dr. Ellis about that. I could not take a chance on his forbidding me to go to the church meeting later. I had to be there. If I depended on my siblings, nothing would ever get done. I was engrossed in my thoughts when Dr. Ellis entered the room. Even though he was in his mid-fifties, he looked ten years younger. He was tall and handsome, with short brown hair and a neatly trimmed mustache. It was a joy having him as my family doctor for so many years.

Dr. Ellis repositioned his eyeglasses which had slid halfway down his nose. He sat on his little black stool and rolled over to the exam table so that he could look me directly in the eye. "And how are you today, young lady?" He teased.

"You'll know once you check my record," I replied, not really wanting to discuss my feeling.

While he was reaching in his coat pocked for his ink pen, I was praying that he wasn't going to do any testing. Today was not the day; I had errands to run. He looked up from my chart and said, "Well, I have good news and bad news. Which do you want first?"

"Give me the good news first," I told him, smiling. "Well, the good news is all your tests from your physical last week were negative. And the bad news, your blood pressure is still elevated, even higher than last week. We have to take care of that right away."

Just to be absolutely sure of the reading, Dr. Ellis took my pressure himself. The reading was the same.

"I'm really concerned about this, Tina Mae, because you haven't had any problems in the past with blood pressure," he said, rubbing his forehead. "I want you to go home and get some rest. Don't do anything that will cause you to over exert yourself; nothing that will cause you stress. Then I want to see you back here Monday morning."

The serious tone of his voice made me uneasy, but I had to remain optimistic. I was not going to accept a diagnosis of hypertension. I knew what was going on in my body and I knew what I had to do to get healthy.

"Dr. Ellis, I've been stressed out lately; my anxiety level has been extremely high. But after tonight, I'll be just fine."

"What about tonight?"

"Oh, it's nothing. I've been doing a great deal of work for the church," I lied. But after tonight, I'll be able to relax."

"Ok, now, I'm going to take your words that you'll get some rest. But I still expect to see you in my office first thing Monday morning, OK?"

"OK. I'll be here bright and early." I will be there as I promised and I felt confident that my pressure will be normal. Why? Because I will no longer be carrying the heavy burden I had been bearing for so long. After tonight, that would be a thing of the past. I left the exam room feeling a little more confident and stopped at the checkout window to make an appointment for Monday morning. I smiled to myself at how crafty I had been in concealing my dizzy episode from Dr. Ellis. Had I told him, surely he would have sent me directly to the hospital. No way was I going for that.

Nothing was going to interfere with my going to that special church meeting. Two years of all my planning was not going down the drain.

The excitement faded. In the back of my mind I felt guilty. Dr. Ellis should have known about the dizzy spell I had encountered earlier. It was a terrifying experience. Quickly I dismissed what happened. "I'll be back to normal after tonight," I said to myself.

I looked for Catherine, but she was nowhere in sight. "She must have been called in the back already," I thought to myself. "If she doesn't call me, I'll call her. I've got to persuade her to be at that meeting tonight!"

* * * * *

I walked out of the office and headed for my black BMW. My husband gave it to me last year for our 29th wedding anniversary, and boy was I proud of that car! To me, it represented prestige and I loved that. I got in and sat there for a moment, contemplating what I should do next. I decided that first, I should contact my siblings to inform them of the dilemma Donald Johnson and Catherine Jenkins had put us in. I know Donald had good intentions and had been terribly frightened by his dream, but a promise is a promise. He should be man enough to live up to his word. And anyway, why was he trying to be so super saved now? Where was his conscious when his family was in distress? Sadly, he was never around when I used to take his wife to see the doctor. And Lord knows he didn't have any conscious when I had to help feed his children when he used to stay out all night with God knows whom. I could not forgive him for what he was about to do to our family.

I took my cell phone out of my purse and called my brother Billy McMann, Jr., the youngest of my four siblings and owner of the law office on Smith Street downtown. Brenda, his secretary answered on the first ring. "Attorney McMann's office," she said softly in her professional voice.

"Brenda, this is Tina. May I speak to my brother?"

"Yes, please hold, Mrs. Black."

"What's up, Sis," Bill said as I sensed apprehension in his voice.

"I don't have time to talk right now, but we need to have an emergency meeting. Be at my house at 4:00 p.m."

"What's going on?" he asked, sounding anxiously.

"You would not believe what Donald Johnson has done! Neither Donald nor his wife is going along with our secret plan any longer. And I just talked to Catherine at the doctor's office. I feel confident that she will renege as well."

"Why do we need to have a family meeting? We can discuss this on the phone? You're just paranoid."

"I'm not paranoid," I almost yelled. "You're the main target of our secret plan. Everything had been centered on you. So contact Sarah and Rebecca and tell them to be there. I don't have time to call them. I'm meeting with Rev. White within the hour. I pray I can still count on him. I am expecting you guys to be at my house at 4:00 p.m.

After a reflective pause, Billy responded, "I'll contact Sarah and Rebecca, and we'll be there."

As soon as Billy had made that promise, he glanced down at his appointment book and realized that he had a 3:00 p.m. appointment.

"Wait a minute, Sis," he said. "I might not be able to make it because I am scheduled to meet with a client at 3:00 p.m.

"You'll just have to cancel that appointment. It's very important that you guys be at my house at 4 o'clock sharp. Our secret plan for the past two years will not go down the drain!"

"Okay, Sis, I'll cancel the remainder of my appointments for today."

I could tell from Billy's tone that he was not too pleased with me, but knew how much effort I had put into this plan. He felt it only fair to do his part to see it through.

"See you guys this afternoon," I said, trying to sound upbeat and light hearted.

I put my phone back into my purse and looked at my watch. I had less than an hour before my meeting with Rev. White.

CHAPTER SIX

Billy sat at his executive desk with his arms folded, staring at the wall in front of him. He was feeling overwhelmed with Tina Mae's secret plan. "How dare her call me, demanding an emergency meeting," he thought aloud.

His eyes shifted to the wall that held his law and theology degrees. Becoming the first lawyer in the McMann family some twenty years ago had been a major accomplishment for him. To say that his parents were excited when he graduated from Durham Law University is putting it mildly. That December morning had been cold and dreary. The snow had started immediately after they had celebrated at Don's Restaurant. They had not come prepared for snow because the weatherman had gotten it wrong, again. And freezing rain on top of the snow certainly had not been in the forecast. Thank God his family had planned to spend the night in a nearby hotel downtown. To travel home in such inclement weather would have been dangerous.

Of course, my father wanted the legacy of the McMann family to remain at Gastonia Church, so he had to entice Bill to attend Mt. Oliver College at night to become a minster, although he had just made the family proud by securing his law degree. My father's plan was to ordain him as the assistant pastor. He was confident that one day Bill would become the pastor of Gastonia Church. Unfortunately, our father died two months before Bill received his degree from Mt. Oliver College. Needless to say, after Rev. Knighton became the pastor, Bill was ordained but never named assistant pastor.

Bill rose from his chair and began pacing the floor. He didn't know what to do. A heavy burden was on his shoulder. Canceling his appointments for most the day was a big deal for him. His clients were important to him, but he didn't want to disappoint Tina Mae. Even though she was paranoid, he knew she had put a lot of effort into planning what was to take place at the meeting. And it all centered on him. He felt obligated to help her, so he walked to his desk and sat back down. Reaching for the phone, he buzzed his secretary.

"Brenda, would you reschedule Mrs. Green's appointment for Monday morning at 8:30 a.m. and if Tina Mae calls, tell her she can reach me on my cell. And by the way, thanks for all you do around here!"

"You're quite welcome, Boss! I'll take care of that right away."

Billy decided to call his sister Sarah first. The phone rang several times before she answered. Sarah had retired three years after Tina Mae. Both had taught at Simpson Elementary School. Sarah was three years younger than Tina Mae. Although Billy had a unique bond with all his siblings, he and Sarah had a closer relationship. Because he was the youngest, she had always been his protector.

"Hello," answered Sarah interrupting his thought.

"Sarah, this is Bill," he said. "Hold on; I'm going to place a conference call with you and Rebecca."

He put Sarah on hold and called Rebecca at her job. She was a social worker at an office in downtown Simpson, a couple of blocks from his office. Rebecca was five years younger than Tina Mae. His mother used to say that Tina Mae and Rebecca were like two peas in a pod.

Rebecca picked up on the first ring. “Good morning, Hanes & Hanes. May I... ”

Bill interrupted her and asked her to hold for a second. And then he pressed the receiver button to retrieve Sarah on the other line. “Are you guys there?” he asked.

“Yes,” Sarah and Rebecca responded in unison.

He let out a loud sigh and then began. “Well guys, Tina Mae called and informed me that Donald will not be at the special church meeting. He's reneged on his promise to help us. And Catherine is iffy. Tina Mae wants to have an emergency meeting at her house at 4:00 p.m.”

“What’s the meeting about?” Sarah asked.

“Is it about Donald and Catherine?” Rebecca wanted to know.

He chuckled. “Your guess is as good as mine,” He said. “I tried to explain to Tina Mae that I had an appointment at 3:00 p.m., but it was apparent that the emergency meeting was more important. She told me to cancel my appointment.”

“You know how Tina Mae gets when she thinks things are not going her way. If our secret plan doesn’t get executed, she might end up in the hospital," Sarah said with a chuckle.

"You're right," Bill agreed, joining her in laughter.

"You guys are absurd, laughing and joking about Tina Mae. I don't think this is funny. Two years ago, Tina Mae initiated our secret plan, and she has relied on our assistance to fulfill our father's wish. If our plan is not executed, it will put the McMann family in an awkward position. We have to maintain our legacy. If not, the church members will have the last laugh," Rebecca said with a hint of disgust. She was, obviously more serious about this than her two siblings.

"Rebecca can't you take a joke?" Bill said.

Rebecca and Tina Mae had similar personalities. They were both aggressive and wanted things to go their way. Rebecca understood Tina Mae's anxiety. She wanted to "win" at the church meeting because she was angry with Rev. Knighton for dismissing her as church secretary and as choir director, and even more importantly, for not naming her brother Billy assistant pastor. After this meeting, she would have the last laugh.

Sarah continued. “Billy, you should tell Tina Mae that you are having some reservations about participating in our secret plan.”

“He should do no such thing!” Rebecca blurted out.

“Hold on Rebecca,” Sarah spoke up. “If that's how he feels, then that's how he feels!”

“But you know that's not right,” Rebecca argued. “For two years, we've been planning this, and now, at the 9th hour, you’re trying to back away. Huh. And Billy, we're doing it for you. I just don't get it!”

“I don’t think so, Rebecca,” Bill objected. “You’re doing it for my father. You know wholeheartedly I didn’t want to be a part of this in the first place. You guys coerced me.”

Sarah cleared her throat, feeling that protector spirit overtakes her. “Billy, you don’t have to go along with this plan if you don’t want to. I will stand behind you all the way.”

“After we have the emergency meeting, if things don’t go my way, I will let Tina Mae know what I am going to do,” Bill assured her.

Rebecca continued to protest. “If you reneged on our secret plan, there’s no reason for us to attend that meeting. Bill you know everything was geared toward you. If you disappoint the family, don't even speak to me again!"

"Rebecca, stop with the pushing," Sarah broke in. "If Bill decides not to participate, we should not pressure him."

"I'll talk to you later, Bill," Rebecca said, "and I expect to see you at the meeting!" And with that she disconnected, leaving her brother and sister to continue their conversation.

"Billy, let Tina know I'll be there and don't be hard on yourself. You make the decision that will best serve you. You know Tina Mae and Rebecca can be overbearing. Love ya much!"

The phone went silent. Bill placed the receiver back on the base, remembering what his mother had always said, "Rebecca and Tina Mae are just like two peas in a pod."

* * * *

Bill's cell phone rang. He figured it was Tina Mae calling to inquire about the meeting. She was the aggressor of the family. What Tina Mae wanted, she usually got.

"Attorney McMann speaking," he said, clearing his voice.

"Hello Bill."

He was relieved; it wasn't Tina. It was Judy, the youngest and prettiest of his siblings, and he was thrilled to hear from her. It had been a while since they had last spoken. Not only was Judy pretty, but she had a personality to match. She was nothing like Bill's other three sisters, and everyone adored her. He began to reflect on how much Judy resembled their mother, with her fair skin and long black wavy hair. Bill, Sarah, and Rebecca were more like their father, with dark skin and high cheekbones.

Although she was quite amiable, Judy was never able to develop a close relationship with her father, mainly because she refused to do anything he asked her to do at Gastonia Church. He had asked her to be in charge of fundraisers, but she had flat out refused. "Father," she said matter-of-factly, "the members are paying the tithe and that should be enough!" When he was fed up her rebellious behavior, he put her out of his house.

Bill thought about the tears that his mother had shed when Judy left home during her senior year in high school. His Aunt Retha, his mother's sister, invited Judy to live with her and her husband Thomas in Atlanta, Georgia, to attend high school there. Their two-story four-bedroom home had more than enough room. The day Judy left, Bill had walked her to the car to say goodbye.

It was then that she had whispered in his ear, "Get away from that old man. He's going to ruin your life!" Judy had been quite successful. She had graduated from college and had become pastor of a mega church in Atlanta. Those words she had said to him so long ago still remained with Bill. Was it possible that she had been right?

Bill drew himself away from his thoughts. "So how've you been?" he asked his sister.

"I'm great," she said, "but I had you on my mind. I just felt like talking to my brother today! What's going on with you?"

"Well, I just got off a conference call with Sarah and Rebecca. We are all scheduled to meet at Tina Mae's house at 4:00. Some of the contacts have withdrawn from our secret plan, so we have to come up with a Plan B because everything has to be intact for the special meeting tonight.

Judy was silent.

"Judy, are you there?" Bill asked after a prolonged silence.

"Yes, I'm here," Judy said finally. "Actually, I'm in town for a workshop. I'm staying at Aunt Minnie's. When I phoned her a few nights ago to tell her I was coming, she told me about this secret plan."

"Is Aunt Minnie still against our going through with it?"

"No, Junior! Aunt Minnie actually told me she had some information that could affect the outcome."

"What kind of information? Did she tell you what it was?"

"Aunt Minnie is carrying a deep dark secret, Junior. Please don't have any part of this plan of Tina Mae's. Go to that meeting at 4:00 and tell Tina Mae that you will not be involved."

Bill respected his sister and knew that she had his best interest at heart, but he didn't want to withdraw without knowing exactly what Aunt Minnie's secret was. He was left with another dilemma.

Aunt Minnie, who was in her mid-seventies and confined to a wheelchair, was suffering from diabetes, and just recently had one of her legs amputated. Two years earlier, she had lost sight in her left eye and hearing in her right ear. She had a multitude of health problems and Bill was not certain that senility was not among them. Should we believe what she says? Could there actually be a secret?

Could Judy have misunderstood her? He knew he had to find out the truth. "God forbid if Aunt Minnie's secret is revealed at the special church meeting," Bill said. "It could be another embarrassment to the McMann family. Remember what happened after dad passed away?"

Bill never did understand why Aunt Minnie had stood silently by and covered for his father's wrongdoing. She had been well aware that he had embezzled $100,000 from the church over a period of five years. He had told her it was for traveling to different conferences and for church equipment, but Aunt Minnie knew better. As her spiritual advisor, Judy had recommended that she explain to the Deacon Board how she had been intimidated by her brother and asked for forgiveness. As a result, Aunt Minnie was not charged with any criminal acts.

Judy had been scheduled to speak at the Convention Center on the north side of town. That was where most of the events were held to accommodate a large crowd.

Bill had mixed feelings. Was he grateful Judy was in town? Was she there to interfere with the secret plan? Aunt Minnie wanted him to withdraw. Why was Judy in town at a conference on the same day of the special church meeting? Bill was sure this was no coincidence. It's no secret they neither Judy nor Aunt Minnie were in favor of their secret plan.

"In ten minutes I have to go back to my meeting," Judy said. "I can't talk long, but don't tell anyone you've talked to me. The workshop will convene at 4:30, and I'll call you and explain everything after I get more information from Aunt Minnie."

"But I'm meeting with Tina at 4:00," Bill said, with a note of urgency.

"I'll call you after 4:30," Judy said with finality," and not a word to Tina Mae about this conversation, and for God's sake, don't make any hasty decisions."

For a moment Bill just sat. He didn't know what to do. His head was spinning. Finally he said, "Your secret is safe with me. I'll wait for your call."

If Aunt Minnie was withholding a deep dark secret, Bill didn't want it revealed at the special church meeting. No way was he going to tell Tina Mae about his conversation with Judy. The two did not get along because Judy would not give in to her intimidation. Tina Mae knew better than to ask Judy to become involved in her secret plan. Bill wanted to take Judy's advice, but at the same time, he didn't want to disappoint Tina Mae.

His back was against the wall. He could not confide in his other siblings; he could not anticipate how they might respond. Bill wanted to call Aunt Minnie, but he knew that if she had not yet told Judy her secret, the chances that she would tell him were slim to none. Why would she withhold a secret and suddenly want to reveal it before the special church meeting tonight? He shook his head.

Bill felt exhausted mentally. Since he had canceled all his appointments for the day, he decided to have lunch and go home.

Bill walked out of his office and paused at the receptionist desk. “Brenda, I’m leaving for the day. I’ll see you Monday morning. Have a good weekend!”

“Thank you, Mr. McMann. Oh, but wait. I almost forgot to tell you that Tina Mae called.”

“Brenda. I told you to have her call me on my cell.”

“I gave her your message,” Brenda explained “but since you were on a conference call, she didn’t want to interrupt. She said she'd call you later.”

“Thanks Brenda. I guess she knew who I was talking to,” Bill mumbled to himself.

As he headed toward the door, Brenda yelled, “See you at church tonight.”

Brenda and her family were members of Gastonia Church, but she didn’t know about the secret plan. “Oh no, if our plan is executed, I don’t know how I will face Brenda Monday morning,” Bill thought to himself.

Bill tried to call Tina Mae on his cell as he walked to his car, but she didn’t answer. He left a message confirming that he would be at her house by 4:00.

Bill just wanted the heavy burden that was on his shoulder to be lifted. How he wished he had never let Tina Mae entice him to be a part of her secret plan. He blamed his dead father for the whole predicament. He was still controlling the family, even from his grave. They had been bewitched into fulfilling his final request. Whatever the outcome, Bill certainly wasn't going to follow in his father's footsteps. He had caused enough embarrassment to the McMann family.

CHAPTER SEVEN

Sitting in my car waiting at Mugel's Restaurant with time to spare, I texted Rev. White to confirm our meeting. Because he was a part of my secret plan, I had to make sure that everything was intact before the special church meeting tonight.

Rev. White had befriended my husband and me shortly after he became a member of Gastonia Church. He appeared to be in his early seventies, with medium build, mixed gray hair, and smooth chocolate skin. He was what the women at Gastonia church would call a "good catch." He was kind and gentle towards my other siblings, but he catered to me, and I often pondered why. Jerome seemed a bit uncomfortable when he was around because Rev. White would grab me by the hand and stare at me with those gorgeous big brown eyes. I think Jerome felt a bit threatened.

Rev. White had relocated to Simpson three years earlier after retiring from the U. S. Army and New Jersey Transit in Newark. His wife had passed away and his extreme loneliness had forced him to come back home. I had often wondered if they had other family members. On several occasions, I had asked if he had any children. He would always change the subject without answering, and tears would well up in his eyes. I thought it strange that he didn't want to talk about his family, so I finally stopped asking.

Rev. White had come by unexpectedly last year and had Christmas with my family. To my surprise, he had only one gift, and that was for me. It was the most expensive gold necklace and matching earrings I had ever received. Of course, I was reluctant to accept the gift without Jerome's approval. Although Jerome barely looked at the gift, he said, "You can accept the gift, but I'm going to keep an eye on that old man."

About two weeks later, Rev. White invited Jerome and me to have dinner with him after the Sunday morning worship service. When I told him that we had other plans, he seemed quite disappointed and insisted on a rain check.

Linda Hopkins, one of my nosey neighbors who was listening at the time blurted out, “I’ll go with you Rev. White!” Then she brushed up against him, flirting. I chuckled. Linda was always trying to get his attention. He just ignored her, however, and walked away.

Rev. White was in disbelief that Rev. Knighton had not appointed him or my brother as assistant pastor at Gastonia Church; so to get back at him, he agreed to assist with our secret plan.

Jerome didn’t approve, however, and told Rev. White that he had not been a member at Gastonia long enough to know what had gone on. In fact, he hadn't even known my father. With Jerome, it was an issue of trust.

I looked at my watch, realizing that Rev. White was late. I decided to go inside, get a table, and wait there. When I got out of my car, I realized that my legs weakened when I tried to stand. Suddenly, the restaurant appeared to be moving away from me. I was having another dizzy spell, so I held on to the opened car door. I was unaware that someone was nearby until I felt a firm hand touch me on my left shoulder. I raised my head slightly and through blurred vision glimpsed someone dressed in a dark blue uniform. A man’s voice asked, “Are you okay lady?”

He helped me back into the car, where I sat trembling. I rested my head against the back of my car seat and closed my eyes until the dizziness subsided. I didn't want to accept that I was having another dizzy spell. It was terrifying not knowing what was happening to me. The man asked again, "Are you okay ma'am? Do I need to call for help?"

I turned my head slightly to the left and saw a policeman standing beside my car door. "No, I'll be okay," I whispered.

The police officer insisted. "I think you need help, lady," he said.

I was grateful that the officer was there to give me a helping hand. But in spite of my distress, I had to convince him not to call for help, especially 911. That would have landed me in a hospital. I had to stay focused. No way was I going to miss my meeting with Rev. White. After all, he was a part of my secret plan. I wanted to make sure we were on the same page before the special meeting tonight.

Quickly I explained, "I'm meeting a friend for lunch. Waving the cell phone that was still in my hand. I texted him about five minutes ago. I was awaiting his call."

"I hope you'll be okay," the police officer said with a concerned tone.

"Thank you. I'm okay. I just left the doctor's office. He said my blood pressure is high. After I've taken my medication, I'll be just fine," I explained.

At that moment, Rev. White drove into the parking lot in his dark blue SUV and approached my car. I blew my horn to get his attention. Pointing with excitement, I told the officer, "That's my friend I'm having lunch with."

"I'll just wait here until your friend parks his vehicle. Are you sure you can drive?"

"Once I take my medication," I lied, "I'll be just fine."

"And please just go away!" I thought to myself.
Rev. White walked over to my car, and the police officer explained to him what had happened to me. "Make sure you take good care of her," he said.

Rev. White seemed confused and hesitant for a moment and then thanked the officer for his assistance.

"Thanks a lot officer," I said a second time. "I'm sure Rev. White will not let anything happen to me."

The policeman looked to him for a nod of assurance and then walked to his squad car and drove away.

"What was that about?" he asked, with a tone of concern.

"We were just having small talk," I lied.

Rev. White was not convinced. "Were you speeding?" He asked jokingly.

"Naw." "Don't be silly! Everything is just fine!"

Changing the subject, I looked at my watch and told him he was late. I didn't like lying to Rev. White and I vowed never to tell another lie after I had executed my secret plan. I chuckled to myself when I remembered that the lie to Rev. White had been my third that day. I had told Dr. Ellis that I was going home and rest. I had told the policeman that I was going to take medication I didn't have. I had to tell a lie about my physical condition. If I told anyone about the dizzy spells I would not be able to attend the special church meeting.

Entering the restaurant, I was greeted by the smell of barbecued ribs. It was the Friday special. My Jerome had worked there as head chef for thirty years before his retirement, and they were still using his recipe. No one could cook ribs like Jerome.

We sat at the back in a booth near the kitchen area. Looking outside the window, I could see that the parking lot was filling up with the lunch crowd.

"Hi there, Mrs. Black," Jessica said, as if surprised to see me. "It's been a while since I've seen you here."

Then she cleared her throat before continuing. "How's Jerome doing? We don't get to see him much now that he has retired. Will he be joining you guys?"

With that, she raised her eyebrows and glared directly at me and then at Rev. White.

I felt my blood begin to boil. "Don't even go there, you gossiper!" I wanted to say. "I'm not fooling around with another man.

"No, Jerome will not be joining us," I said in a tone to let her know that I did not appreciate her insinuation. "But he knows I'm here. And By the way, I'd like a take-out of his favorite dish, the ribs with mashed potato and green beans."

In an effort to clear the air, I continued, "Jessica, I'd like you to meet Rev. White. He's a member at my church and a friend of the family."

Jessica flipped her long braid over her shoulder and extended her right hand. With a more mellow tone she said, “It’s a pleasure to meet you Rev. White.”

Rev. White stood smiling and reached for her hand. “The pleasure is all mine,” he said, obviously enjoying the moment.

“So you’re a member of Gastonia Church, too. I heard bout y’all's special meeting tonight. Everybody in Simpson is talking about it. My mother and father will be there. You know I don’t belong to that church no more. I left three years ago. Not a day too soon,” she laughed.

“What have you heard about the meeting?” I interrupted.

“Oh- nothing much,” she laughed again. “I hope she doesn’t know about our secret plan,” I thought. “But if she knew, she would have told everyone in this restaurant and I would have heard it by now.”

Jessica popped her chewing gum and took the pad out of her black and white uniform pocket to take our order.

“What can I get you guys to drink?” She asked, placing the menus on the table.

"Water," we both responded in unison, but Rev. White requested lemon slices as well.

Rev. White and I both ordered the special of today. Snapping his fingers to get Jessica's attention as she headed for the kitchen, Rev. White said," And please put Tina's order on my ticket."

Jessica's eyes widened. I could tell that her mind was returning to the gutter.

"Your orders will be out shortly," she said over her shoulder.

Rev. White leaned forward in his seat and whispered, "So Tina, what do you want to talk about? Why did you want me to meet you here? You sounded urgent on the phone. Is everything okay?"

"Before I discussed why you're here, I have to share this with you. Donald Johnson came by the house this morning. He has withdrawn from our secret plan."

"Withdrawn? Why?"

"He said he had a dream that something was trying to take me away at our special church meeting, and no one could protect me. I've never seen him that nervous before. The way he was acting, it was as if I had asked him to rob a bank. He thinks the dream was a warning and that

I should not execute our plan. But I just think he was having a nightmare."

Rev. White stroked his chin as if contemplating what to say, but I continued.

"But my main concern is about our agreement, Rev. White. I'm meeting with you to discuss what progress you've made with the ministerial staff."

"Well, I kinda wanted to talk to you about that, too," he said with a reluctance that made me a little nervous.

By that time, Jessica was back.

"Here are your orders," she said, winking at Rev. White. "I told you guys I'd be back shortly. Mrs. Black gets special treatment round her. Her husband was one of our best cooks ever. Can I get you guys anything else?"

"No thank you," the two of us responded in unison. After Jessica walked away, Rev. White continued.

"Tina, I'm not sure if I can go along with this plan of yours."

I stopped sipping my water and glared directly at him. "Wait one minute, Rev. White! Please don't tell me that you're going to renege, too. I was counting on you to rally the support of the ministerial staff!"

I lifted my eyes upward as if to see them and began to count the preachers in Gastonia Church. "Let's see, six, seven, we have eight ministers, Rev. White, and we need the support from at least six of them."

Rev. White's eyes saddened and then he spoke. "Tina, everyone had originally agreed to go along with your plan, but when I spoke to Rev. Jenkins yesterday, well, he withdrew. And I think he must have influenced Rev. Thomas, Rev. Berry, and Rev. James because they have all asked me to give you their regrets. That's why I was late arriving here. I was on the phone with Rev. Jenkins, trying to get him to change his mind."

"I wanted an explanation Rev. White. Why are you and the other ministers trying to sabotage my plan?"

Rev. White wiped his mouth with the napkin and then paused before speaking, trying to choose his words carefully.

"Listen, Tina, I've given this a lot of thought. Maybe you shouldn't execute your plan. I agree with Donald; his dream could have been a warning."

I know he could see the fire in my eyes.

"So you've been talking to Donald about this?" I accused.

"No, Tina, I haven't," he said. "But there is something I need to tell you."

"Well tell me, Rev. White!" I said a little too loudly.

By that time Jessica was back with my take-out order. I had a sneaky suspicion that she had been trying all along to determine what we were talking about.

"Mrs. Black, here's your take out. Good seeing you again. And Tell Jerome not to be a stranger. We miss him around here!"

Then she turned her attention to Rev. White, handing him the bill. "It was nice meeting you. Please don't let this be your last time dining with us. You can pay at the counter on your way out."

Rev. White nodded and Jessica left us. "Tina, I know you are upset, but we have to keep this quiet. You can't allow your emotions to get out of control. You must keep your voice down!"

I could tell that he was afraid that Jessica had heard some of our conversation. But at the moment, that was the least of my worries.

"No! I won't keep my voice down," I said. "You promised me two years ago that the ministerial staff would support me with our secret plan and now you're saying you don't think it's a good idea. What's wrong with you? Are you afraid of Rev. Knighton? It's not like he's going to appoint you as the assistant pastor. Have you been talking to him? I'm sure he's behind everything that is going on. That man has taken positions away from everyone in my family. He must pay for what he has done!"

"Tina, please don't make a scene," Rev. White whispered, "Everyone is watching us."

"I honestly don't care about that right now," I told him. "I just need to know why everyone is reneging right here at the last moment!"

"I am not reneging, Tina. I just don't have the support of the ministers. And anyway, there's something else you need to know before the meeting."

"Oh, so there's more?" Suddenly, I didn't feel very well. The knots in my stomach were tightening, and I felt light headed. I inhaled a deep breath, praying that I was not about to experience another dizzy spell.

It was about that time that Rev. White nodded toward to the restaurant entrance and whispered, "Two of our members just walked in, Rev. Phillips and his wife. I think we'd better leave. I don't want any rumors about us being together."

"What about our plan? Are you in or not?"

"I'll call you Tina and we can discuss it further over the phone before the meeting this evening."

I sat there speechless for a moment. I didn't know what to do. Three of the main lay members as well as four ministers had all decided that they were not going to live up to their promises. I was glad I had called an emergency meeting with my siblings to come up with a plan B.

Rev. White stood first to leave. He looked down at me and said, "Don't worry, Tina. I have another plan. We can discuss it when I call you later. "

With those words, Rev. White left quickly before Rev. Phillip or his wife could see him. They had been seated on the opposite side of the restaurant, so I turned slightly so that they could not be able to recognize me. I could not muster the strength to leave just yet. I was trying to figure out why everything seemed to be falling apart. I didn't understand why no one seemed to understand my rationale for correcting the obvious wrongs of Rev. Knighton. After I sat there a moment and gathered myself, I could feel my confidence returning. In spite of what Rev. White had told me, I still felt that my father's request was going to be accomplished successfully. I just had to stay focused.

Before I stood to leave, I prayed, "Please God don't let me have another dizzy spell."

THE VOICE

I knew the Voice had said no more interruptions for a while, but I wanted to know if my secret plan had been executed before I had embarked upon this journey of sorts. So again, I abruptly stopped reviewing my Book of Life and pleaded.

"Please, Sir, can you just tell me if my plan was executed! What did Rev. White have to tell me? I don't want to do this anymore!"

"You have no other choice," the Voice thundered at me. "You will abide by MY will. Continue!"

CHAPTER EIGHT

Friday afternoon I walked into the church secretary's office unannounced. I was there because she had informed me that Rev. Knighton had said that there would be no agendas at the special church meeting, and I wanted to know why.

"I'd like to speak to Rev. Knighton," I told Carrie, standing in front of her desk. Her eyes widened as if I had asked to see the President of the United States.

She looked down at her appointment book and then back to me.

"I can't seem to find your name," she said. "Did you schedule an appointment?"

"No, I did not!" I retorted, feeling myself getting a little perturbed with her. "But it's important that I speak to Rev. Knighton before the special church meeting tonight!"

"I'm sorry Mrs. Black, but he's not here. He's already left for the day."

"Left for today?" I repeated. "Well, can you reach him?" I asked, thinking, "The church isn't paying him to goof off."

"I am so sorry, but he has asked not to be disturbed."

"He should have left a number," I muttered. I didn't know what to do. Rev. Knighton wasn't in the office, and I had no way of knowing the order of the meeting. I had headed for the door, but then turned abruptly and asked Carrie if she had any idea as to the meeting agenda. Of course she told me that she did not. Whether or not that was the truth I would never know.

I was mystified. I wondered if anyone had revealed to him my secret plan and whether that information had prompted him to change the order of the meeting. I had told the Deacons that I wanted my name on the agenda, so I decided at that very moment that if my name was not there, I would simply interrupt the meeting and reveal my plan. I vowed to have my say.

Before leaving, I looked around at the remodeling in the secretary's office. Even though I had disagreed with the cost, the Deacon Board just ignored my input. "If my father had been alive, that never would have happened," I thought to myself," and after tonight, Carrie won't be sitting behind that desk."

Standing in the doorway, I could feel my nose begin to tingle because of the overpowering scent of fresh paint emanating from across the hall. "Carrie I'm going to take a look around the church," I told her. I wanted to see the other remodeling that had been done. Because of the unprecedented growth in the membership, Deacon Brown had recommended to the Deacon Board that the Fellowship Hall be expanded and that all classrooms be painted.

I walked through the building, assessing the work that had been done, shaking my head in disgust all the while. I knew they had spent monies unnecessarily, and I would voice my opinion to the Board at the special meeting tonight.

I stopped in the door way of one of the classrooms for just a second, closing my eyes. I could hear the echo of my father's voice, "The church doesn't need all those repairs."

"After tonight," I whispered to my dead father, "there will be some changes at Gastonia Church. Rev. Knighton's days had been numbered."

The clock on the wall of the fellowship hall read 2:00 p.m., and I wanted to shout for joy. In five hours, the McMann's family secret plan will be executed.

I walked back into secretary's office. To my surprise, Rev. Jenkins was sitting next to Carrie's desk. I was yearning to speak to him about withdrawing from my secret plan, but not in front of Carrie. Besides, I had to wait for Rev. White's call. He said there was something else I needed to know. So I just put it on hold to speak with him later.

I was curious to know why Rev. Jenkins was sitting in Carrie's office. Was he there to speak with Rev. Knighton? But Carrie had said he was gone for the day. Would he dare divulge our secret plan to anyone before the meeting? I could not be sure, but I certainly hoped he wasn't. But he seemed unusually "cool" toward me. We had been friends for many years and usually talked non-stop when we met. There was something different about today, so I was determined to find out what it was. I just walked over where he was sitting and greeted him.

Standing about six feet tall, Rev. Jenkins extended his right hand, his face curving into a half smile. Then he said, "Hi, Tina Mae! What brings you here?"

I just picked up my purse from the desk and stared him down. Then I walked away, and looking over my shoulder, I said, "I'll see you at the church meeting tonight."

He only nodded. He did not have to be a mind reader to know why I had chosen not converse with him. We both knew what was up.

Before getting into the car, I took my cell phone out of my purse to check my messages. I had missed two calls, so I stood beside the car and retrieved the first message. It was Rev. White saying that I should call him right away. It sounded urgent.

Hastening, I returned his call. There was no answer, so I left a message asking him to get in touch with me before 4:00 p.m. It was very important that I talk to him before my siblings arrived for our meeting.

Before retrieving the second message, I put my cell phone on speaker. Listening to Catherine babbling, I was agitated. "Dr. Ellis has recommended rest as the best cure for the flu," she said, "so I'd better do what he said."

I knew it! She would not be attending the meeting tonight. I put my phone back into my purse and stood beside my car for a moment, pondering. I wanted reassurance about Catherine's illness. I had to know if she was really telling me the truth, so I turned around to go back inside the church to speak with Rev. Jenkins. If Catherine wasn't really ill, maybe he would be able to tell my why she was withdrawing her support from our plan. Before I reached the door, I began having second thoughts. "Why bother with Catherine?" I asked myself. "After all, she did have a terrible cough when I saw her at the doctor's office. And maybe she does have the flu. Anyway, I'll have enough contacts.

I got into my car and drove home, feeling a little frustrated that Rev. Knighton had not been in the office. With no printed agenda for the church meeting and I was clueless about whether the four ministers had revealed my secret plan to him. I was fidgeting. I wanted to call the ministers before the special meeting, especially Rev. Jenkins, my friend, but I felt that my hands were tied.

Trying to clear my head, I listened to my favorite gospel program on WWOO Radio Station. When I heard the DJ reading my announcement, I couldn't help but smile. I turned up the volume in time to hear him say "There will be a special church meeting held at Gastonia Church Friday night at 7:00 p.m. All members please attend." Then he added, "Now y'all that's my church, and we're going to re-elect the Rev. Arnold Knighton as pastor tonight."

"That's what you think!" I heard myself saying aloud.

* * * *

I was sitting on my favorite love seat relaxing before meeting with my siblings. Jerome came into the den with a piece of barbecued rib in his hand. Licking his fingers, he said, "Hi Baby, Rev. White called trying to reach you. Ump these ribs are almost as good as the ones I cook. And he said he'll call back at 4:00 p.m."

"Oh no, that's not going to work," I told him. "My siblings will be here by then for the emergency meeting. I have to speak to him before 4:00."

Jerome looked somewhat bewildered. "What emergency meeting?" he asked. "I didn't know anything about a meeting."

He wiped his hands with a napkin and then he sat down beside me on the sofa.

"Well, some of my contacts have withdrawn from my secret plan," I told him. "So I told my siblings to meet here for an emergency meeting at 4:00 p.m. We need to discuss Plan B before the special meeting tonight."

"Who has withdrawn besides Donald?" Jerome said, picking his teeth.

"Rev. White told me at our meeting that four ministers have withdrawn - Rev. Jenkins, Rev. Berry, Rev. James, and Rev. Thomas, and Catherine Jenkins has the flu. The doctor has told her to get some rest. But at the doctor's office today, she was acting rather strange. She was about to tell me why she wasn't going to attend. But the nurse called me to the examination room."

When Jerome realized that both Rev. Jenkins and Catherine had withdrawn, his expression showed deep concern. They were our friends. As a matter of fact, we had gone out for dinner together last week and neither had mentioned anything about withdrawing from my secret plan.

Jerome picked up the telephone to call Rev. Jenkins. "I am his friend," he said with a tinge of anger. "He should've told me. I want to know what's going on."

"No, Jerome," I said, grabbing his arm. "Put the phone down. Rev. White told me there was something else he needed to explain. I'm sure it's about why the other ministers have changed their minds."

"What about Rev. White? Is he still a part of your plan?"

"I'm not sure. That's why he called."

"Tina, do you think you can pull this off?" Jerome seemed really worried.

"Yes, Jerome. You don't have anything to worry about. After I meet with my siblings, we will finalize Plan B. And anyway, Rev. White told me not to worry because he had another plan, too."

"I told you I was keeping an eye on that old man. I don't trust him."

"What do you mean you don't trust him? He had been nothing but nice to me since he came to Gastonia Church."

"Quite frankly, he's been too nice."

I chuckled. Jerome was jealous.

"Well, he didn't explain why the four ministers withdrew from your plan, did he? It's apparent that he's withholding information that could affect you."

I could tell that Jerome wanted to get to the bottom of the situation, so I thought it'd be best that I call Rev. White.

"Tina did you hear me?" he asked.

"Yes, I heard you, dear, but I think you're blowing things out of proportion."

"Seriously, Tina if all your contacts don't have your back, your secret plan will be a disaster. You need their support."

"Don't worry, Jerome. Two years of planning will not go down the drain. I've got everything under control. You just wait and see. My father's request will be executed."

"Tina, is that all you're concerned about, your father's request? You know I'll stand behind you, but I really don't want to be a part of a plan that is doomed to fail.

I had always been able to depend on my husband's support, so it concerned me that he was concerned. I had to reassure him that we could pull this off.

"Jerome, I promise that I'll have enough contacts to execute my plan. You've got to trust me."

Raising his eyebrow, Jerome rose up off the sofa to go upstairs. With a serious look on his face, he said, "Tina, just let me know when your siblings arrive."

Trying to absorb the conversation I had with my husband, I decided to call Rev. White. I didn't want to wait for his call. It was 3:45 p.m.

As I reached to dial his number, I saw the flashing red light which indicated that I had a new message. I pressed the button and immediately heard Aunt Minnie's faint voice.

"Tina Mae," she said, barely audible, "this is Aunt Minnie. Please call me before the meeting tonight. It's very important. I need to speak to you about Rev. White."

I looked around to make sure that Jerome had not come back downstairs. I certainly didn't want him to hear what Aunt Minnie had said. When I was certain that he was still upstairs, I quickly dialed Aunt Minnie's number. And, of course, she did not answer. Instead, it was her health care provider.

"Miss Minnie can't come to the phone right now, Miss Tina," she said. "She's taking a nap. The medication I gave her makes her drowsy. Can I have her call you when she wakes up?"

What was I to say, except, "Yes." I didn't know what to do. I needed to know why Aunt Minnie had called me. But I would have to wait. I couldn't fathom not trusting Rev. White. We had a developed such a close relationship. If Aunt Minnie did not call soon, it would be too late. Rev. White would have to explain. I still had time to call him before my 4:00 meeting.

Quickly, I dialed his number. He answered on the first ring. "Rev. White, this is Tina Mae. My husband gave me your message, but I need to speak with you before 4:00 p.m."

"I was about to call you Tina," he said in a tone that was just a little too calm. "I'm sorry I had to leave the restaurant all of sudden."

"Rev. White, I don't have long to talk. Could you just tell me what else I need to know?"

"Listen, Tina, you should withdraw from this plan of yours," he said very matter-of-factly.

"Withdraw from my secret plan? But why?"

"I think it would be better if I came over to your house to explain."

"Come to my house? Are you stalling?"

"No, Tina! I just think it would be better if I speak with you in person."

"Rev. White, what are you talking about? Does it have anything to do with the four ministers withdrawing from my plan?"

"Well, yes, in a manner of speaking," he admitted.

"Did they reveal my secret plan to Rev. Knighton?"

"Tina. Please. What I have to say is important. I could be at your house in five minutes. I need to speak with you and Jerome right away."

I knew that would not be a pretty scene. Jerome had already said he did not trust the man. "By the way, your Aunt Minnie will be calling you," he continued. "Please let me come over before you speak with her."

"As of matter of fact, Aunt Minnie called while I was out. I just returned her call, but she was napping. And I left a message for her to return my call. But wait a minute. Aunt Minnie isn't a part of our plan. Why did she call me?"

I felt myself getting flustered because Rev. White was not answering my questions. He just continued to say how important it was for him to come over to speak with Jerome and me in person.

"You can't come over here," I told him firmly.

If he was stabbing me in the back, I didn't want him knowing I was meeting with my siblings.

"Rev. White, I need to talk to Jerome to see if it's OK for you to come over. I'll have to call you back," I told him, trying not to sound too agitated.

As I turned, I saw that Jerome had come back downstairs. He stuck his head in the den door and mumbled, "Your siblings are here."

"But I didn't hear the doorbell ring," I told him.

"I know, I saw them getting out of the car from the upstairs window."

Before the doorbell rang, I hurriedly told Jerome about my conversation with Rev. White. I could see anger rising in him.

"He told you to withdraw from your secret plan? After all this time, are you kidding me? I don't want that man in my house, Tina. I will not meet with him. Whatever he had to say to you, he should have told you on the phone. Why does he have to speak to both of us anyway?"

"Jerome, Please. We need to know what else he has to say before the meeting tonight."

"No, Tina! He's waited until a few hours before the meeting to tell you to withdraw from your plan. He's playing games. I will not meet with him."

I stood there speechless. I didn't know what to say. Maybe Jerome was right. Rev. White was playing games. He couldn't be trusted. He should've explained what he had to say on the phone. I would just have to await Aunt Minnie's call, but I had no intention of mentioning to Jerome whatever Aunt Minnie was going to tell me. If he knew that Rev. White had involved Aunt Minnie in this, he would be furious. I had to keep that to myself.

I have been planning for this day for two years, in spite of the obstacles; I would not let my father down. My siblings were here, so I had to focus on plan B. I still had enough contacts to execute my secret plan without the assistance of Rev. White or the other four ministers.

THE VOICE

The thundering sound was echoing all around me. "Tina Mae Black," the Voice announced, "from this point on, you will fully understand why you're here."

"Please tell me if my secret plan was revealed. Why did four ministers renege? And what did Rev. White have to tell me? They must have talked to Rev. Knighton. Can you just tell me what happened? It's obvious I don't deserve to be here. So far I haven't seen anything that can't be forgiven."

The Voice responded with such a thundering sound that I jumped. "Tina Mae Black, I'm still in control. You must abide by my will. Continue reviewing your Book of Life."

CHAPTER NINE

My siblings were sitting on the sofa anxiously waiting for the meeting to start. But I didn't want to begin without Jerome. He had gone to the kitchen to get sodas for everyone. I reached for the contact list that I had placed on the end table earlier. I wanted to share it with my siblings. It contained pertinent information to help us execute our plan. For two years, I had protected it like a mother hen.

Before sitting down, I removed the family portrait that was placed in the center of the fireplace mantel. I was grateful that my father had left it in my care after my mother passed away. In the photo, Bill and Sarah were standing on the right side. Judy was standing in the center. Rebecca and I were standing on the left side behind my mother and father.

For a moment, I held the portrait in my hands, staring at Judy. Even though she was my sibling, I had not sought her assistance in executing our plan. She and I had never gotten along. She never agreed with any of our father's decisions. But my focus was not on Judy. After all, the meeting was about my father, so I placed the portrait back on the mantle and took a seat.

Jerome entered the room with a tray of sodas and placed it on the glass coffee table in front of the sofa. Then he walked to his favorite chair near the window and took his seat. Staring at me he said, “Let’s get this meeting started.”

I began the meeting by telling my siblings about Donald’s dream and his belief that it was a warning. Then I told them that he had withdrawn his support.

In unison, Bill and Sarah said, “Wow!”

“Now, I know you guys don’t believe that the dream was a warning. It was just a nightmare. Jerome and I laughed at him. There’s no way I’ll be taking out of the church meeting by some unknown force. The assertion is ridiculous. I will not let a dream interfere with my father’s wish. Are y'all with me?”

Bill rubbed his forehead. "I don't know, Tina. It sounds like he might have had a premonition to me."

"Did he explain what took you away?" Sarah wanted to know.

"No, Sarah!" I shouted, with my agitation taking over.

Rebecca turned and looked at Bill and then Sarah. Agreeing with me, she said, "That wasn't a warning. Being a part of the McMann's secret plan had generated stress. He was fearful."

"Well, sometime dreams come true," Bill said. "Two years ago, I dreamed that I was involved in a hit and run car accident. Three days later while driving my red truck on Main Street, I was hit from behind, and the culprit left the scene. The impact totaled my truck. Fortunately, I was able to describe the man and the vehicle that hit me and he was apprehended."

When I made no comment, Bill changed the subject. "Is Catherine coming to the meeting this evening?"

"No, she isn't," I told him. "She called earlier and left a message saying that the doctor wanted her to rest."

All of a sudden, things became crystal clear to me. Catherine must have known that Rev. Jenkins had withdrawn his support. That explained why she had exhibited such strange behavior at the doctor's office. But I really could not understand why Catherine had not confided in me. After all, we had become close friends. I was confident that Rev. White was in the middle of all of this.

Donald was beginning to see the light as well. I could hear the frustration in his voice when he asked whether Rev. White and the other associate ministers would be at the meeting that evening.

"No, ah yes, ah well, I'm really not sure," I said.

"What exactly are you saying, Tina Mae?" Bill asked, obviously exasperated.

"Well, Rev. White told me earlier today that he and the other four associates wanted to withdraw their support," I explained.

"Well, did he say why?" Sarah wanted to know.

"No, not really. He implied that there was something else I needed to know, and he asked if he could come over to speak with Jerome and me but..."

"But I told Tina not to trust him." Jerome interrupted. "He's just trying to sabotage her plan."

"Tina, you should talk to him," Sara said, talking to me but staring at Jerome. "It might be important. It's crucial that we know what he has to say before we continue with this plan of ours."

Rebecca, who had been relatively silent until now, put in her two cents worth. "I never trusted that man either."

"Tina, call Rev. White back right now," Bill said. "I want to know if he has revealed our plan to Rev. Knighton."

"No," Jerome shouted. "I don't trust that man. End of discussion!"

Jerome's tone was so loud and authoritative that my siblings were spell bound. No one uttered a word. I could have heard a pin drop.

Jerome was right. After I spoke with Aunt Minnie, the truth would be revealed about Rev. White. If he had told Rev. Knighton about my family's plan, it still would not stop me. I still had enough contacts to assist us.

Bill looked at his watch. "Tina Mae, time is of the essence. Donald, Catherine, and four ministers have withdrawn. I say that we need to discuss Plan B. How many contacts do we have to assist us?"

While Bill was reviewing the list I gave him, I explained, "We had five hundred members on the roster at Gastonia Church. In the past two years, I have contacted three hundred. I'm sure we will have at least two hundred members attending the special church meeting."

"But over half of these members were reinstated when Rev. Knighton became pastor. They're not going against him! How do you think you're going to pull this off?"

"Most of the contacts on that list are members, yes, but they don't regularly attend."

For a moment, Bill sat there puzzled. He was mesmerized by the amount of work I had done in contacting so many members to solicit their support for our plan.

No way, I'm going to tell you or anyone else how I enticed those members to be a part of our secret plan, especially Jerome. I chose the members who only attend church Easter, Christmas, weddings, or funerals. The method I had used to get most of my contacts to assist me was nothing short of bribery. I don't like the word but that is exactly what I used. Realizing that some of the members were experiencing financial problems, I had offered my assistance. Instead of paying me back, they agreed to be a part of my family's secret plan. For instance, when Mrs. Franklin was behind on her rent, I offered to pay it for her. In return, she agreed to assist me with my secret plan. For other contacts, I had paid their rent or car payments, bought food, and even paid to keep their sons out of jail. But the scary thing is that I had not told Jerome that I had taken $20,000 out of our retirement fund to be able to offer such assistance. He had trusted me with the bookkeeping. I just prayed he would never find out that the money is missing.

My contacts had not been made aware of the whole truth. I had only told them that I needed their help to assure that the McMann family legacy will stay intact at Gastonia Church, and they had promised to vote my family back into our positions of power. So when I revealed the truth about Rev. Knighton's relationship with Deacon Brown at tonight's meeting, I felt confident that they would have my back.

My contacts can read between the lines. I didn't have concrete proof, but it doesn't take a rocket scientist to figure out what's going on when two males are always together, and neither is ever seen with a female companion, especially when both are quite handsome and could have the "pick of the litter."

I felt very confident that when Rev. Knighton's true character was revealed at the meeting tonight, the McMann Family would regain the legacy of Gastonia Church. Without a doubt, my contacts would stand behind me all the way.

Snapping back to the original question my brother had asked me, I said, "Oh, it was easy to get the list. I simply told the church secretary that I needed the names and addresses of all the active and inactive members so that I could invite them to our homecoming service."

"You did what?" Sarah frowned. "Tina, you're incorrigible!"

"It's no big deal, Sarah. Anyway, I did ask Joyce Green if I could assist with the homecoming committee. I worked with her three years ago. Remember? Besides, I told you guys to just assist me and I would do all the planning. So did you guys contact the members I asked of you?"

"Yes, we did," Sarah said proudly, "and they'll be at the meeting."

I turned to Rebecca, who nodded in affirmation.

"Good! So now it's time we put our heads together for Plan B."

Bill's phone buzzed and he looked at the clock. A frown appeared on his face.

"Is something wrong?" I inquired.

"Oh no, it was a text I was expecting, but it wasn't the answer I was hoping for."

"Is it a client, Sarah asked?"

"Well,"

"Who was it Bill?" I pressed.

Bill began fidgeting and seemed suddenly impatient.

"I'll take care of it after the meeting. Tina, let's just finish. We have to get ready for the meeting tonight. We only have a few hours."

I wondered if he was withholding pertinent information that would affect our plan, but I didn't dare ask. I had to stay focused. Finally, our father's wish would soon be executed. The McMann family was going to regain the legacy of Gastonia church.

Bill stood and walked over near the mantle as if contemplating his next question.

"OK, Tina Mae, since I'm the main target, how will you present our secret plan to Rev. Knighton and the members tonight?"

"It's quite simple," I told him. "Our father wanted you to become the next pastor after he passed away, but you hadn't yet been ordained. Now you have, so when the election is held tonight, I'm nominating you as pastor. Rev. Knighton thinks that he will be running without opposition, but he is in for a huge shock. And you have nothing to fear. Two hundred members will vote in your favor. They've promised me that I can count on their support to put the McManns back in power!"

"Yea, but they didn't know they would be voting to make me Pastor," Bill argued. "I just pray they won't disagree with what we're trying to do."

"Don't worry, Bill," I reassured him. "That won't be a problem. I have everything under control."

My mind went back to the money I have freely given those who needed it and the juicy gossip I would share about the unsavory relationship between Rev. Knighton and Deacon Brown. After learning about that, the congregation would gladly prefer Bill over Rev. Knighton.

Nervously, Bill said, “But what if…”

“No what ifs,” I interrupted him. “I've done my homework. I've got this in the bag! I can’t wait to see the expression on Rev. Knighton's face when you become the next pastor of Gastonia Church!”

“My main concern is the members,” Bill continued as if he had not heard a word I had said. “What is they won't give me the respect they've given to Rev. Knighton. And besides, I won't have any Associate Ministers. They've all withdrawn from our plan, remember? That says to me that they support Rev. Knighton. This is a heavy burden, Tina Mae. I don't know if I want to be in charge of Gastonia Church!”

“Listen, Bill,” I said, almost yelling, “We've been over this for two years. You've known my plan all along. I shouldn’t have to keep explaining every detail. There’s nothing to fear. Once you’re elected the members' hands will be tied. The McMann will be back in control and there’s nothing anyone will be able to do about it, not even Rev. Knighton.”

Bill starred at Sarah; they both appeared worried. Bill was silent for a few minutes, and then he sighed. “Okay, Sis,” he conceded, “I just pray everything goes as planned.”

Toning down my voice, I again assured my brother that all would be well. But there were other pressing issues that had to be brought to the table. I had planned to nominate Rev. White as Assistant Pastor, but if he was withdrawing his support of the plan, we had to choose someone else.

“Bill, can you think of someone trustworthy to be nominated as your Assistant?”

This all had to be finalized before the meeting. There could be no slip-ups. But Bill had tuned us all out. He simply was no longer focusing. “We'll deal with that later, Sis,” he said as if in a daze.

Ignoring him, I continued. “Rebecca, it's my plan to have you voted back in as Church Secretary. You know you held that position for fifteen years, prior to Rev. Knighton's coming on the scene and replacing you with Deacon Brown's niece, Carrie. And Sarah, I plan to reinstate you as Chair of the Ushers Ministry. Who could be more qualified than you? After all, you did it for eighteen years before

Rev. Knighton replaced you with Deacon Miller's wife. So what if the ushers claimed you were too controlling? What do they know?"

Bill massaged his temples as an obvious means of relieving stress. Then came the obvious statement.

"Tina Mae, you haven't told me what you want to do. Yes, you were the Choir Director for twenty years, but please tell me you're not considering returning to that position. After you were voted out, over twenty-five members joined the choir, and we're still counting. I don't think they'll appreciate having you back, especially those musicians who returned after you were voted out. Y'all just couldn't get along."

"Well, I've decided that I'm not interested in being choir director. I'm still hoping Catherine Johnson will take that position. I plan to appoint myself as chairperson of the Trustee Board. We need someone to oversee the finances. Lord knows the way they've been spending money, we might be heading toward bankruptcy."

Bill looked at Jerome and then back at me. "Tina Mae, after I become the pastor, I will make Jerome Chairman of the Deacon Board and he will replace Deacon Brown. And since Donald won't be replacing Deacon

Murphy as the assistant chairman, have Jerome decide who he wants as his assistant."

"But Jerome won't have time to find a replacement. That's why I'm so upset with Donald for withdrawing his support right here at the last minute. You see, according to our by-laws, someone has to fill that position the night of the election."

Jerome had held that position of chairman of the Deacon Board for over twenty years prior to Rev. Knighton's arrival. That is why it had never been clear to me why Rev. Knighton had removed him and appointed Deacon Brown anyway. It had to have something to do with their close relationship.

"If you ask me," Rebecca blurted out, "I just know Deacon Parker would be suitable for that position. He gets along well with all the members. Don't you agree, Jerome?"

Jerome scratched his head, contemplating her recommendation. "Well, I guess it's a good idea," he said, "but I'd prefer my cousin Donald." He paused and thought for a minute more. "Bill," he continued, "I guess Deacon Parker would be a good assistant. After all, he was dissatisfied when I was no longer the chairman. You can appoint him."

Bill nodded in affirmation. I looked at my husband and then back to my siblings. Finally, I said, "So we have a Plan B, but we still don't know the order of the meeting. Rev. Knighton told me that there would no agenda. I went by the church on my way home to confront him, but he wasn't there.

"We really don't need an agenda," Bill said. "After Rev. Knighton starts the meeting, then we will know what to do."

"When the deacon starts the election," I said, I'll stand and have my say."

Finally, we could all breathe a sigh of relief. Everything was settled for the meeting. But a thought weighed heavily on my mind. Why would Aunt Minnie call me about Rev. White? I didn't want to tell my siblings until I spoke to her. Looking at my watch, I still had time to call her before getting dressed.

Bill's cell phone buzzed again interrupting my thought. His face lit up like a Christmas tree. "I have to answer this call," Bill said rushing out of the den. "I will see you guys at the church tonight." All my siblings rose to leave at the same time.

While Jerome was upstairs freshening up for the church meeting, I called Aunt Minnie again. The home health care provider told me she was still asleep. I sat there for a moment. How badly I wanted to know what she had to tell me about Rev. White. I didn't know what to do, so I just repeated the same message, "I'll call her back within the hour if I haven't heard from her."

I sat on the sofa staring into space trying to put two and two together. Suddenly I remembered what had happened two weeks ago after the Sunday morning worship service. When I introduced Rev. White to Aunt Minnie, she didn't extend her hand. Instead she looked at him and rolled her eyes and said harshly, "I know who you are." Rev. White made no comment. He simply stood there starring at her.

Aunt Minnie told her aide to please take her to the car, so she pushed her away in the wheelchair. "I'll call you later, Tina Mae," Aunt Minnie has said over her shoulder. At the time, I wondered what was going on, what her connection to Rev. White could possibly have been. Maybe they had had a fling back in the day. But why would Aunt

Minnie wait until the night of my secret plan to call me about him?

When I told Aunt Minnie that Rev. White was assisting with my secret plan, she tried to warn me. "Even though he has agreed to help you," she said, "I doubt he'll keep his promise." I trusted him, so I just ignored that statement, assuming it was just animosity between the two of them.

Although Aunt Minnie was upset about the McMann legacy being taken away, she wasn't pleased with my secret plan. Aunt Minnie told me to pray. "Things will work out for the McMann family," she would always tell me. You see, Aunt Minnie always acknowledged her role in the McMann Family being ousted from positions of power in the church. I, on the other hand, was not so willing to take responsibility.

"Tina Mae," Aunt Minnie would say, "You should ask yourself why you were voted out. I blame myself for what I did, and you should do likewise. And God has forgiven me."

I was not going to listen to that nonsense. In my head, Rev. Knighton was responsible for the shift in power, and I was going to do whatever it took to get it back.

I needed answers. I couldn't just ask Rev. White to come over because Jerome refused to speak with him. It was apparent that Aunt Minnie knew why he wanted to withdraw from our plan. I had a couple of hours to freshen up and get dressed. I didn't dare be late. My father's favorite words kept ringing in my ears, "Come hell or high water, I am going to be on time."

For two years, I had waited for that special night to vote my brother in as pastor of Gastonia Church. I was sure Aunt Minnie would call me before the church meeting. I went upstairs to change clothes.

THE VOICE

The Voice had said that this part of reviewing my Book of Life was crucial, so I didn't ask questions. Meeting with my siblings was not unusual, and I didn't see anything wrong with my wanting to maintain the McMann legacy at Gastonia Church. Trying to fulfill my father's request certainly was not a sin. After all, my family had been in positions of power at Gastonia Church since 1835.

CHAPTER TEN

On his way upstairs, Bill didn't see Cherice and Diandrea sitting at the kitchen island. He was so engrossed in his thoughts that his wife startled him when she spoke. Twirling spaghetti around her fork, she wanted to know if he was going to eat dinner. As much as he liked spaghetti, tossed salad, garlic bread, and Italian dressing, he wasn't hungry.

Butterflies had invaded his stomach ever since the meeting with his siblings. He appreciated Cherice's thoughtfulness in picking up take-out so they would not be late for the meeting, but he simply could not eat.

Bill walked over and kissed his wife on the cheek. "Wow!" Cherice looks as beautiful as she did the day they met twenty-three years ago. He began to reminisce about their initial meeting. He had been having lunch in the cafeteria while attending Duke University, when he looked up and saw her standing in front of him, staring at him with her big brown eyes. She had the body and face of a fashion model, and he was simply spellbound. "Excuse me," she had said with a smile, "but can you give me directions to the library?" He told her he was going that way after he finished his lunch and the rest is history.

Next Bill walked around the kitchen island to embrace Diandrea. She lit up like a Christmas tree, for after all, she was a daddy's girl. Bill often tells Diandrea she resembles her mother; tall, beautiful brown eyes and light complexion.

Diandrea was a junior at D.H. Conley High School on the south side of town. "Daddy, our school won in Track and Field Day today!" she told him excitedly.

Bill winked at Cherice and told Diandrea how proud he was of her.

"One day our daughter is going to run as fast as Mariann Jones," he said to his wife as she nodded with a chuckle. Then he excused himself to upstairs to freshen up for the church meeting.

No way was Bill going to explain to Cherice about the emergency meeting he had had with his siblings. Even though she knew he was the only McMann who could possibly maintain the legacy of Gastonia Church, she had begged him not to support our secret plan. Cherice had been constant in her plea for the McMann family to drop their ridiculous vendetta against Rev. Knighton. "He has not mistreated the McMann Family," she had insisted. "He's been nice to all the members at Gastonia Church, and y'all need to let this McMann legacy thing go!"

Although he did not want to disappoint his family, Bill had major reservations about becoming the pastor. Serving as First Lady would be an uncomfortable position for Cherice. Just yesterday she had told him that she had no desire to assume that role. For years she had served on the Deaconess Ministry and was highly respected by all the members. She didn't want to change that.

Bill disliked going against his wife. They had always been able to work together on any situation. But because Gastonia Church had been in the family since 1865, our father had requested that the McMann legacy be maintained. And since he was the only McMann that was a minister, he had to step up to the plate. He couldn't disappoint his father. But at the same time, he wanted to please his wife. It was an impossible situation.

"Oh God," he cried out in anguish, "What have my father and Tina Mae gotten me into? I don't know what to do."

Bill sat down on his bed and reached for the phone on the night stand, but then he hesitated. Cherice or Diandrea might get a phone call and he didn't want his call disturbed. He decided to use his cell phone instead. He was stressed and needed to talk to someone about his dilemma. Bill closed the bedroom door so that no one would be able to hear his conversation and dialed Sarah's number. He knew she would have his back. Sarah answered on the first ring. "Bill is that you?"

"Yes," he whispered. "Well, why are you whispering?" Sarah asked in that reassuring tone that he needed to hear.

Clearing his throat, he continued whispering, "I don't want Cherice to hear our conversation. I've got some disturbing information I have to discuss with you."

"What disturbing information? What are you talking about? Are you ill Bill?"

"No."

Sarah was getting excited. "OK, tell me what's wrong. Had you decided to withdraw from our secret plan?"

"I don't know what I'm going to do, Sarah. Judy is in town. She doesn't want anyone to know she's here. Please don't say anything to Tina or Rebecca. You're the only one I can talk to."

"Judy is in town? Why?" Sarah asked, her voice pitch rising slightly.

"She called me this morning and said she had to speak at a workshop at the Convention Center. And she also told me that our secret plan could be in jeopardy at the special church meeting tonight."

"What do you mean there might be a problem? What kind of problem?"

"Judy told me that Aunt Minnie is carrying a deep dark secret. And it could affect our secret plan. I don't know what to do, Sarah."

"We have to tell Tina and Rebecca," Sarah explained.

"No! We can't," he said. "Judy begged me not to say anything to anyone, especially Tina and Rebecca. It was Judy texting Bill at our emergency meeting. She told him that Aunt Minnie was sleeping."

"Sleeping? Aunt Minnie's not feeling well? If she's ill how can she tell us anything?"

"Don't worry, Sarah. Let's just wait for Judy to call back," Bill said trying to reassure her. "I'm sure everything will be taken care of before the meeting tonight,"

"Bill, what are we going to do about the meeting tonight?"

"I don't know what to do," he repeated. My wife wants me to withdraw immediately. That's why I called you, Sarah."

"Withdraw immediately?" Judy had been sensitive about our secret plan from day one.

"I suggest you not make any decisions until Judy speaks to Aunt Minnie and gets back to you."

Sarah was silent for just a moment, and then she added,

"Although I have twin boys, neither of them is capable of pastoring a church. Allen is on drugs and Mark is still away at college. Tina Mae doesn't have any boys. And Judy and Rebecca don't have any children at all. It's up to your family to keep the legacy going."

"I know," Bill responded reluctantly. "But we don't need to worry about that right now. Our main concern is about tonight. I'm not sure we can trust Aunt Minnie. I know you remember what our father did to her. Although she never retaliated, she must have been furious at the time. She just might be using this opportunity to get back at him through us. I don't want any embarrassment tonight!"

"Why didn't you contact me earlier?" Sarah asked. "We could've had a Plan C."

"The only thing we can do for now is await Judy call. I'll let you know as soon as I hear from her."

Bill looked at his watch. It was 6:12 p.m. The special church meeting was scheduled to start at 7:00. He decided that if he didn't get a call from Judy by 6:30 he would call her. His instinct was telling him that Aunt Minnie was planning to show up at the church meeting, and that would be devastating.

When Cherice came into the bedroom to get dressed for the church meeting, Bill lowered his voice and told Sarah he would have to hang up. He could not allow Cherice to know what was truly about to take place. She walked over to the closet flipping through her clothes and took out his favorite knee length black dress. Bill had purchased it last month from Macy for her 40th birthday.

"So, who was that on the phone?" she asked, raising her eyebrows awaiting an answer.

Bill didn't know what to say. He hated lying to his wife. He just wanted to walk over and give his wife a hug and tell her what was going on. If it were a problem other than the secret plan, she would have told him exactly how to handle it. She was full of Godly wisdom. Bill looked toward the ceiling as he heard the lie come out of his mouth.

"No one important. It was just my sister Sarah."

"What did she want?" Cherice pressed.

"She wanted to have prayer with me before I go to the church meeting," he lied. He interrupted Cherice with small talk before she could ask any more questions. But to tell the true, he wanted to get on his knees and pray. He just knew he was going to need all the prayer he could get.

After taking a quick shower, Bill walked to the guest bedroom and retrieved his black suit from the closet. The closet in their bedroom was overrun with Cherice's clothes, so there was no room for his. He then walked back to their bedroom and stood in front of the mirror to button his white shirt and find a matching tie. Tina Mae had told him to dress to impress, so he didn't want to disappoint her.

The bathroom was adjacent to the bedroom. Bill walked inside and looked into the mirror once more to brush his short black hair. He admired his reflection. He actually looked like a minister on the outside, but inside he could hear Judy's voice echoing, "Withdraw, Withdraw, Withdraw."

When the phone in the bedroom rang, Bill was startled back to reality. Both he and Cherice reached for it at the same time, but he decided it would be better to let Cherice answer it because his heart was pounding so loudly that he was sure both she and the caller would be able to hear it. If it was Judy, he hoped Cherice would not ask her a lot of questions. He had already made up his mind to tell his wife everything after the meeting. He could no longer live with the secrecy; he loved his wife and wanted to be totally honest with her, no matter the outcome.

When Bill realized that the call was for Cherice, he breathed a sigh of relief. Her supervisor at Welcome Hospital, where she had worked for many years, was calling to request that she report to work to fill in for a nurse who had called in sick. The smile on Cherice's face indicated that she would not have to leave for work right away. In fact, she would be needed the next day, so she would be able to support her husband at the special church meeting.

Bill was still anxious about Aunt Minnie's deep dark secret. In a weak moment, he considered confiding in Cherice, but then he decided against that, thinking that she might change her mind about attending the meeting. Instead, he would just have faith and hope that everything would go as planned. He went downstairs to wait for her to finish getting dressed. He didn't rush her as he normally would because he wanted to be alone to speak with Judy when or if she called.

As soon as he was settled on the sofa, the phone rang. Bill answered it and was disappointed to find that it was Sarah and not Judy. He could tell that the anxiety of waiting to hear from Judy was getting to Sarah. He could hear it in her voice.

"Bill, we've only got half an hour before the meeting," she said. "I think you need to call Judy. We've known all along that neither she nor Aunt Minnie is in favor of our plan. We can't keep waiting. It seems to me like they're playing games. We can't afford to be late. Call them and get back to me!"

Sarah was right and Bill knew he had to do something. They needed answers. The clock was ticking like a time bomb.

"I'll call her," Bill agreed. "Hang up. I'll call you back."

Just as Bill was about to dial Judy, she called, apologizing for not having called earlier. "I still can't get the full story from Aunt Minnie," she said. "She has only been able to give me bits and pieces because she was still drowsy from her medication. And on top of that, her words were slurred, but she did mention Rev. White."

"Rev. White?" Bill interrupted. "What did he do, Judy? Will it have any effect on our secret plan? Will he be at the meeting?"

"Please control yourself, Junior," Judy said, sensing that Bill was allowing his apprehension to get the best of him. Then she continued. "Aunt Minnie told me that Rev. White was blackmailing our father."

"Blackmailing our father? But Why? I thought it was the other way around."

"I don't know why. She hasn't told me everything. I told you that the medication is not out of her system. I've been looking thought some of Dad's old files trying to find information to corroborate Aunt Minnie's story, but I haven't found anything yet. When she's fully awaking, I can tell you more. Aunt Minnie also mentioned that she wanted to speak with Tina Mae. But in the meantime, Bill, I would withdraw from this secret plan."

Bill thought about what Tina Mae had told them earlier that day at the emergency meeting about Rev. White.

"Rev. White called Tina Mae today and wanted to come by the house to speak with her and Jerome. But Jerome refused because he doesn't trust him. I need to speak with Tina Mae, NOW! She didn't say anything about Aunt Minnie calling her. I don't want to be embarrassed at that meeting tonight!"

"Please don't call Tina Mae," Judy pleaded. "We don't know why Aunt Minnie wants to speak with her. And you know how aggressive she can be, blowing everything out of proportion. Bill, I'm warning you, I'm begging you to withdraw from this plan. In fact, if I were you, I would not even go to the meeting."

"Judy, I have no other choice but to go to the meeting. If Rev. White was blackmailing our father, I don't see how that could have any effect on our secret plan. Are you sure Aunt Minnie is not hallucinating? The medication she's taking could be too strong."

Bill was obviously frustrated. He didn't want to hear any more about Rev. White. None of it was making any sense. Knowing he had to leave or be late for the meeting, he ended the conversation.

* * * * *

Bill and Cherice reached the church about twenty minutes before the meeting was set to begin. He told his wife to go ahead inside so that he could have a few minutes alone. Cherice complied, thinking he might need a moment for prayer. Actually, Bill was too numb to move at the moment. He was felt as if the weight of the world rested on his shoulders. He took out his cell phone and called Sarah to let her know the latest. She became hysterical when he told her that Aunt Minnie had murmured something about Rev. White having blackmailed their father.

"That's ridiculous," she almost yelled. "And anyway, what connection could there possibly be between this supposed blackmail and our secret plan? Weren't you going to appoint Rev. White as your assistant pastor? This is all so crazy! Much obliged to Tina Mae for not revealing our primary secret to him. I say we go ahead with our plan and forget about Rev. White. If Aunt Minnie can wake up out of her medical stupor and call Tina Mae, then she will inform us what to do. If not, Oh well!"

"But what if Aunt Minnie shows up at the meeting?" Bill continued. He was not so sure that everything was truly under control. His nerves were shot. He had more to lose here than anyone else. Suddenly he had a thought. "Sarah," he said, "I'm going to call Tina Mae!"

He put Sarah on hold and pressed the flash button. Tina Mae's phone rang six times, but no one answered. He clicked back to Sarah to let her know he had had no luck in reaching Tina Mae. "I'm here in the church yard already, but I don't see her car. I guess she must be on her way."

"It's apparent that Aunt Minnie has spoken to Tina Mae," Sarah said. "I assure you that it's not that important. Tina Mae would have informed us if it had been. We don't want to be late. You go ahead inside. I'll be there in a couple of minutes."

"OKAY, but I've asked Judy to text me if she finds out anything we need to know right away. I pray that she has just blown things out of proportion because she is against our plan."

CHAPTER ELEVEN

Deacon Brown was a bit apprehensive about the upcoming Deacons' meeting set for 6:00 p.m. and even more so about the special members meeting set for 7:00 p.m. As he got into his car to head for Gastonia Church, his cell phone rang. He glanced quickly at the screen and saw that it was Rev. Knighton. It was 5:43 p.m., only seventeen minutes before the Deacons' meeting was set to begin. Knowing Rev. Knighton's hectic schedule, Deacon Brown thought he might be calling to inform him that he was going to be late. But instead, Rev. Knighton was calling to expresses his regret that he would not be able to attend because "something important had come up."

Carrie had informed him that Tina Mae had come by the church earlier in the afternoon insisting on having an agenda for the meeting tonight. Rev. Knighton was not going to tolerate Tina Mae's take-over spirit, so he had come up with a plan, which he had left on his desk in a manila envelope. He wanted Deacon Brown to retrieve the envelope and explain the plan to the Deacons at their 6:00 p.m. meeting.

Deacon Brown started his ignition and sped off. "That Tina Mae is always causing trouble," he said out loud. "No matter what, she wants things to go her way. I am fed up with her fighting with Rev. Knighton. She might as well get over it. Rev. Knighton is the pastor of Gastonia Church, and there's nothing she can do about it!"

Deacon Brown had gone on with his tirade to himself long enough. He wished he had the courage to say to Tina Mae everything he had just said to himself. It was because of her that Rev. Knighton had been secretive about his attending classes in preparation for the ministry, all in the name of keeping the peace. To say that he was sick of it would be putting it mildly.

When Deacon Brown reached the church and headed for the pastor's office, it dawned on him what Rev. Knighton might have in that envelope. He had been certain that Rev. Knighton was planning to appoint him as the assistant pastor. That had to be why Rev. Knighton had insisted that he attend Bible College. Oh, there was no doubt in his mind that God had called him to preach, but he had kept that secret to himself. He simply didn't feel ready to take on a task of such magnitude. He had not yet reached that "Send me; I'll go" point in his life.

It would have been wonderful if the other Deacons could have known about his calling and his Bible college attendance; their moral support would have given him the courage he needed to walk in his calling. But because of Tina Mae, all of it had to be kept in the dark. Had she known, she would have made Rev. Knighton's life a living hell. After all, her brother was a McMann, and in her narrow mind, Rev. Knighton should have been promoting him. He would just wait and see what the meeting revealed.

Before heading to the conference room, Deacon Brown went into the pastor's office and retrieved the envelope Rev. Knighton had told him about. He didn't want anyone seeing him leaving, so he quickly closed the door and took the few steps to the conference room next door. He took a seat and waited the arrival of the other Deacons. His curiosity got the best of him, so he decided to open the envelope.

To his surprise, inside the envelope were copies of a letter with instructions as to when it was to be distributed. After speed-reading to the last paragraph, he heard himself say aloud, "Not another secret! I can't do that! I'm not ready for that!"

"Not ready for what?" Deacon Murphy said, entering the conference room. "Boy that must be some letter you're reading. Is everything okay?"

"Well, yes, everything's fine" Deacon Brown lied. "I guess I got carried away."

He quickly placed the envelope into his briefcase. He couldn't chance Deacon Murphy's getting a glimpse of what was on the letter, not just yet. It was to be the last item on the agenda for their meeting. He stood up to greet him, giving him a firm handshake. Deacon Murphy was the assistant chairman of the Deacon Board, but Deacon Brown decided that he had better follow Rev. Knighton's directive to the letter.

Deacon Brown was glad the other Deacons were arriving so that Deacon Murphy would not have an opportunity to question him further about the letter. He made it a point to greet everyone and inquire about their day, just so that there would be no lull in the conversation until he could start the meeting.

Deacon Brown glanced at the clock and saw that it was already 6:08 p.m. He had to get the meeting started so that they would be out in time for the special meeting at 7:00 p.m. They had a lot to discuss, but mainly he wanted to be free of the secret he had been required to keep for so long. It had become too much of a burden for him.

Deacon Brown called the meeting to order and asked Deacon Murphy to render an opening prayer. Then he continued. "Well gentlemen," he said nervously, "I'm sure you're wondering why this meeting has been called, so I'll get right to the business at hand. Rev. Knighton allowed me to meet with you because there's something very important that you need to know about me."

He could tell that he had their undivided attention. In fact, the intensity of their expressions made him a little uneasy. But he continued. "I just hope you all will forgive me."

At the moment he said that, Deacon Brown remembered the rumor that Tina Mae had circulated about him and Rev. Knighton and their supposed homosexual affair. He knew he'd better clear that up right away.

"And let me go ahead and clear this up right now. What I have to tell you has nothing to do with my being a homosexual. I know about the rumor Tina Mae has been circulating. That is an outright lie. Trust me; I'm straight. In fact, I am engaged to be married."

"Well, thank you Jesus," Deacon Murphy laughed. "And who is this special lady?"

"You'll meet her soon enough," Deacon Brown smiled back before continuing. "I wanted you all to know two years ago, I started studying to go into the ministry. Rev. Knighton plans to present me to the congregation tonight as a candidate for ordination. He felt that you all should know and he hopes that he has your support.

Deacon Brown was amazed that the Deacons were all very thrilled at his revelation. They stood and shook his hand one by one. Deacon Murphy was the last deacon to shake his hand and give him a bear hug.

"Man, you should have told us," he said. "You know we would have supported you!"

"I really wanted to," Deacon Brown replied, "but with Tina Mae's husband being on the board, I couldn't chance letting my right hand know what my left was doing. He would definitely have told Tina Mae, and she would have done whatever she could to interfere."

"You're right, Deacon Brown. Deacon Black would have revealed your secret to Tina Mae and she would have caused trouble for you."

Then Deacon Murphy glanced around the conference room, as if just realizing that all of the Deacons were not present. "So where are Deacon Black and Deacon Johnson anyway? Why are they not attending this meeting?"

"Well, Deacon Johnson said he wouldn't be attending this meeting or the special meeting later. He sounded really troubled when he called and wants to speak with me tomorrow. And Deacon Black told me he had something important to do with Tina Mae, but if he gets done in time, he'll stop by. If not, he wants me to tell him what we discuss. He is planning to be at the 7:00 p.m. meeting."

"Now, Deacon Brown, you know how Tina Mae always tells him what to do," Deacon Murphy joked. "If she had known about this meeting, she would have been here herself. As a matter of fact, she has been very adamant that all the deacons be present at the special church meeting tonight. That woman has something up her sleeve!"

They all roared with laughter. But Deacon Brown's face became serious.

"Come on, guys," he said. "We've got to get back to business. I'm grateful to have your support, but what about the membership? Do you think they'll accept me? I know Tina Mae is going to rebel against it. She'll probably have a heart attack!"

Deacon Murphy started laughing again. "Relax, Deacon Brown," he reassured him. "The members will accept you. And as far as Tina Mae is concerned, there's nothing she can do. You've completed your training, so step into your calling. We've been giving that busy body way too much power!"

Deacon Murphy was quiet for a moment, and then he continued. "Tina Mae is still bitter because the members voted her out as Choir Director. I pray she doesn't act like a maniac at the meeting tonight like she did at our last election. She kept jumping up and down saying that Rev. Knighton and our Deacon Board were not acting in accordance to the By-Laws. I cringed in my seat when she pointed her finger at Rev. Knighton, accused him of being responsible for her being voted out as Choir Director, and threatened him by saying 'You'll pay for this.'"

Tina Mae had caused trouble for everyone seated around the conference table. He stared at Deacon James sitting opposite him and remembered how Tina Mae had threatened him with being replaced as Superintendent of the Sunday school, a position he had held for many years. After her father's death, Tina Mae had even gone to Rev. Knighton to encourage him to replace Deacon James, but Rev. Knighton had not listened to her, thank God.

Deacon Little spoke up, recalling the time he had escorted Tina Mae out of the sanctuary during a call meeting. She had made a huge scene because Carrie had replaced her sister Rebecca as Church Secretary. On her way out, she had warned Carrie that she wouldn't hold that position more than two years. He recalled thinking that Tina Mae's reaction was like Satan having a temper tantrum when he can't have it his way.

The reminiscing went on for a few more minutes. Deacon Murphy reminded Deacon Miller what Tina Mae had told his wife when she replaced her sister Sarah as chairperson of the Usher Ministry. It had been the same "You won't be in this position but two years" warning she had given to others.

Realizing that their meeting needed to conclude, Deacon Murphy again spoke, "I could have done the holy dance when Tina Mae's little brother Bill didn't become the pastor after his father passed away. Thank God he wasn't ordained at the time. If he had been, Lord have mercy, we would've been stuck with another McMann. He would've done everything Tina Mae told him to do. This church would not have prospered. It's sad, you know. Rev. McMann intimidated his entire family, all but Judy, that is. And she left home. And his wife, God rest her soul, she was so afraid of him that she just allowed him to push her around. She was such a sweet lady. I know she went to Heaven, but Rev. McMann? The jury is still out on that."

"Deacon Murphy, please!" Deacon Brown chuckled. "Let's get back to business at hand and stop gossiping."

"Okay, Deacon Brown, you're right, but just let me say this," Deacon Murphy continued. "Deacon Parker is the elder of all us Deacons. He will be seventy-five his next birthday. Tina Mae disrespected him. Although he was her husband's close friend, she still tried to get him removed from the Deacon Board, saying that he was too old. That woman is a force to be reckoned with!"

Deacon Parker and Deacon Matthews were nodding approval, so Deacon Murphy would not stop.

"And you, Deacon Matthews, Tina Mae and her family stopped being your patients. They started going to another dentist right next door to you. She retaliated just because you told her in the last call meeting that her family had tried to run Gastonia Church since its establishment in 1865 and that they would try to get rid of anyone who crossed them. That was what prompted her decision not to patronize your business."

It really had become obvious that Tina Mae had negatively affected the lives of every person in that room.

"I'm so glad Rev. Knighton does not allow that family to boss him," Deacon Murphy said. "I'm so glad he's our pastor, because under him, things have changed. I've been a member here for thirty years, but the last two years have been the best ever. Tina Mae and I have never gotten along. I went to school with her and she was aggressive, even way back then. Rev. McMann let that gal do whatever she wanted to, so she ran the church. And that's why she thinks she can still run it now! But after tonight, well, after Deacon Brown's secret is revealed, you guys had better run for the door. She's likely to kill us all."

Deacon Blakely scratched his forehead then he looked at Deacon Murphy and said, "Are you saying I need to go and get my 45?" Deacon Blakely never took anything seriously. He was just on the Deacon Board for the ride.

"Deacon Blakely, this is the Lord's house!" Deacon Brown shouted.

"Just joking, just joking," he said. "I don't even have a 45."

Deacon Brown looked at the clock that was placed on the wall over Deacon Murphy's head. He exhaled a loud sigh. It was 6:44 p.m. The special church meeting was staring in five minutes.

Deacon Brown was grateful for the support of the Deacons, but he still had to explain the letter inside the envelope that Rev. Knighton had left. He wanted to speak to Rev. Knighton first because he had no intention of doing what his pastor was requesting of him. Apprehensively, Deacon Brown held up the envelope and said to the Deacons, "I know we only have a few more minutes, but there is one more thing I need to tell you this evening. It is something I was not aware of until I arrived here and got this envelope from Rev. Knighton's office."

With that said, he distributed copies of the letter, and as they read, the laughing and joking ceased and their smiles were replaced with shock.

Deacon Murphy was the first to speak. "Well gentlemen," he said, "looks like the ball is in Deacon Brown's court. Now we just have to convince the members. If this is what Rev. Knighton wants, I guess we have no other choice."

Deacon Brown didn't know what to say. He glanced around the conference room and realized that everyone was staring at him, waiting for an answer. A heavy burden was on his shoulders. "I need more time" is all he could manage to utter.

"I know this is a surprise to you just as well as it is to the rest of us. But Deacon Brown, we need an answer before we face those members. What are you going to do?"

"Right now, I'm going to Rev. Knighton's office and discuss this with him," Deacon Brown told him. "Then I'll make my decision."

Suddenly, there was a tap on the door. It was Carrie letting Deacon Brown know that Rev. Knighton was in his office and had requested to see him before the meeting.

"Let him know that I'm on my way," he said before giving a brief closing prayer and adjourning the Deacon's meeting.

Deacon Brown walked to the side door and glanced out before heading for Rev. Knighton's office. The parking lot was crowded with cars, the way it looked only when there was a funeral at Gastonia Church. Deacon Brown was frightened. This crowd meant that something was amiss; he just didn't know what.

Deacon Brown walked to Rev. Knighton's door, and just as he reached for the knob, Deacon Murphy touched his shoulder and whispered, "Everyone knows Tina Mae had the special church meeting announced on the radio. And it was advertised in the newspaper. Don't worry; we've got your back!"

Deacon Brown paused briefly before opening the door and whispered a prayer.

"Dear God, please help me present my plans to the members of Gastonia Church. I know they are going to be shocked, but don't let any weapon that is formed against me prosper. Amen."

CHAPTER TWELVE

"Where are you going in such a hurry," I asked Jerome as he headed for the bedroom door. He looked quite handsome in his black suit and tie. But the suspicious look on his face concerned me.

"I'm going next door to speak with Donald," he mumbled. "Hopefully, I can persuade him to reconsider and be a part of your secret plan. Quite frankly, I'd really prefer him as my assistant over Deacon Parker."

"Why waste your time with Donald?" "I'm sure his mind is made up, especially after what he said this morning about the dream, or nightmare, or whatever it was."

"There's no harm in trying one more time. Maybe I'll be able to talk some sense into him."

"Please don't bother, Jerome. It's far more important that you speak to Rev. White. He's the one we need to be concerned about. Besides, he's awaiting my call. I didn't let him know whether he could come over to speak with us."

Jerome stopped dead in his tracks and turned around to face me. "I told you that man is not trustworthy. He just wants to come over to apologize, but it's a little too late for that. He knew before tonight that he wasn't going to participate in your plan. I will not discuss anything with him, and that's final."

"Okay, Jerome, but don't say I didn't warn you. What if he comes to the special meeting tonight and reveals something that could hurt our plan?"

"There's nothing he can reveal, Tina. It's not like he's going to explain to Rev. Knighton that he at first had agreed to help you. And anyway, the only reason he agreed was to get close to you."

"Why bother talking to this man about that?" I said to myself. "He's just insanely jealous, But I'm going to call Rev. White anyway, just as soon as he leaves."

"We have about an hour before the meeting," he said, looking at his watch. "You sure you want to go through with this?"

“Yes Jerome, for the umpteenth time! I've got this! I know I can pull this off. Rev. Knighton will not get over on me tonight. It’s not going to happen!”

“I hope you understand that it’s going to be difficult, especially with your not having an agenda. Had it not been for your emergency meeting with our siblings, I could have gone to the Deacon's meeting earlier. I'm sure they were informed about the meeting format.”

“With or without an agenda, I have everything under control. Like I told you guys at our meeting, it’s simple. I'll just ask to speak before Rev. Knighton is re-elected, and then I'll nominate my brother Bill as the next pastor of Gastonia church. There you have it; my secret plan will be revealed.

“Tina, it’s not that simple. Rev. Knighton is going to object.”

“So what if he objects? My 200 contacts will be there to support me!” I thought to myself that they had better support me, because I had given them all various sums of money.

“I'll wait for you downstairs after I speak with Donald. And please hurry! I don't want to be late!” With that directive, Jerome headed downstairs.

I didn't want to focus on Donald. I had other things to consider, mainly, Rev. White.

After I freshened up, I walked over to my closet. I wanted to choose the perfect outfit. Tonight was special, so I wanted to look my best. I chose my blue and white pantsuit I picked out earlier today. I had paid a lot of money for it, and it exuded class and quality. It would be perfect. Then I walked over to my floor model jewelry armoire and paused. I wanted to accessorize my suit with the matching gold necklace and earrings that Rev. White had given me, but I knew that doing so would infuriate Jerome. I decided that his feelings didn't matter, not on this night, so I put them on anyway.

As I stood there admiring myself in the mirror, I decided I'd better make one last attempt to call Rev. White before heading downstairs. I dialed his number, but it went straight to voice mail. He was playing games with me, and I didn't like it one little bit.

"He doesn't know who he's playing with!" I thought to myself. I picked up my contact list and stuck it into my purse. I would use it to check roll. I definitely wanted a record of those in attendance. Then I took a few minutes to rehearse in my mind what I was going to say at the special meeting. My thoughts were interrupted when my cell phone rang. I thought it must be Rev. White, but Aunt Minnie's name appeared. I had been so focused on Rev. White and the special meeting that I had forgotten all about Aunt Minnie.

Excited, I answered and heard her faint voice say, "Tina Mae is that you?"

"Yes Aunt Minnie. I tried to reach you earlier. I got your message. And Rev. White called, too. Do you know why he wants to speak to me?"

"Yes, Tina Mae. Please don't go to that special church meeting tonight. Rev. White might embarrass the McMann family."

"Aunt Minnie the church meeting will be starting in a few minutes. Can you just hurry and tell me what this is all about?"

"Okay, Tina Mae, but I must warn you, you're not going to like what I have to say. Rev. White was blackmailing your father, and I have proof of that!"

I started feeling sick to my stomach, so I held onto the bed post.

"Are you sure, Aunt Minnie?"

"Yes," she replied. "I'm one hundred percent sure."

"But how do you know? What proof do you have?"

"When I was the church financial secretary, your father sent huge sums of money to Rev. White. I knew it wasn't for church business, so I questioned him about it. That's when my brother told me what was going on and then begged me not to tell the church. He promised to pay back every penny. I never told anyone because I loved my brother, and I just couldn't let him down. So when the members asked for a financial report, I would always come up with an excuse. I would say that I didn't have the bank statement, or I would just make up figures to show that our church account was in good standing."

"I'm sorry Aunt Minnie, but I just don't believe my father would let anyone blackmail him. Did he say why he was giving the money to Rev. White?"

"He just said he would explain it to me one day. But that day never came. He took that secret with him to his grave. God rest his soul."

"Was Rev. White aware that you knew he was blackmailing my father?"

"No. Well, not until your father passed away and I approached him and threatened to tell the Deacons. That's when he told me that if I told, it would affect your secret plan."

"Is that why he wants to speak with me before the meeting? Is he planning to come clean?"

"Yes, because I threatened to tell you if he didn't."

"How can you be so sure he will reveal this at the special meeting tonight? And what does it have to do with my secret plan?"

"Think Tina Mae. If your secret plan revolves around your father, and Rev. White knew something about your father that enabled him to get away with blackmailing him, then your plan could certainly be in jeopardy."

"Well, I've been calling him, but I haven't been able to reach him. Aunt Minnie, I will not let Rev. White or anyone else interfere with my plan. I've waited for this much too long to allow anyone to spoil it. And anyway, I just don't believe him. Jerome always said he was not trustworthy. I'm sorry but, I know my father. That $100,000 was not blackmail money. I don't see the connection. Furthermore, Rev. White willingly became a part of my secret plan after my father passed away."

"Tina Mae, please listen to me. Don't go to that meeting tonight," she repeated. "He also mentioned that Rev. Knighton . . ."

With that, Aunt Minnie's voice began fading, or was I losing consciousness? The phone was slipping out of my hand, and I could feel my legs giving away. Somehow I was able to get to my bed and sit on the edge. By then my head was spinning and the room became dark. I was experiencing another dizzy spell.

"Oh no, this can't be happening to me again!" I thought.

I needed help, but I couldn't speak. And even if I could have, Jerome wouldn't have heard me. He had not yet returned from Donald's.

The dizzy spell seemed more serious than the other two. Slowly, I rested my head on a pillow, too afraid to move. It seemed like forever before I regained control. When I tried rising up off the pillow, I experienced severe heart palpitations. My breathing was labored and sweat was pouring off my face. When I tried to wipe it away, I realized that my hands were shaking uncontrollably. For the first time, I actually began to regret that I had not followed Dr. Ellis' orders to go home and rest. He had warned me that my blood pressure was out of control, but I had put the meeting before my health. What a huge mistake!

Finally, I was able to compose myself and slowly sit up. When I saw my cell phone lying on the floor, I remembered that I had been talking to Aunt Minnie. I was sure she would be worried and wondering what had happened during our conversation to make me end it so abruptly. As I felt myself returning to normal, I remembered that Aunt Minnie had mentioned Rev. Knighton before my episode. I knew I needed to call her back, but when I checked my watch, I knew I didn't have time. At that very moment, Jerome appeared in the doorway and startled me.

"Tina Mae, I told you to be downstairs when I got back. It's time to go."

Then he walked over to the bed where I was still sitting and surveyed me closely.

"You look pale," he said. "Are you alright? You look like you've seen a ghost. Why are you holding your phone? Did you get an upsetting call or something?"

He was asking way too many questions.

"Jerome, I'm okay," I lied.

"Then why are you sitting there holding your phone?" he asked again. "Who were you talking to?"

"No one! I took the phone out of my other purse. I wanted to make sure to take it with me."

"I don't believe you, Tina. When I came in here, the expression on your face showed stress and anxiety. I know you!"

"I just got upset because I was looking for an earring," I continued to lie, and I had a hard time finding it because it blended in with the carpet."

It was at that point that Jerome actually looked at my jewelry choice and realized that I had chosen to wear the gift from Rev. White.

"So, I guess you were upset because you thought you had lost the set Rev. White gave you?" he asked with obvious disgust.

"No Jerome. I was upset because it cost more than what I normally pay for jewelry. That's why I was anxious to find it."

Jerome bought my lie and sat down beside me on the bed. He stared into my eyes and said lovingly, "Tina, you don't look too good."

The sweating had subsided but had not completely stopped, so Jerome took my hand and begged, “If you’re not feeling well, let's not go to the special church meeting. I'll stay home with you. You are far more important to me than any special meeting.”

He gently touched my forehead and then quickly got up to get the thermometer from the bathroom cabinet to take my temperature.

“I don’t have a temperature, Babe,” I said, trying to sound convincing. “It’s probably just a hot flash. I’m okay, really! We've got only twenty minutes to get to the church. You go start the car. I'm going to wash my face and grab my jacket. I'll be down in a second. I'm just fine.”

After he left the bedroom, I was too afraid to move. I didn't want my movement to trigger another spell. As I waited to make sure I could stand, I whispered a prayer and then texted Bill, asking him and Rebecca to meet me outside the church. Then I headed for the bathroom to wash my face. I would not have time to redo my makeup. But Jerome had always told me that I looked good without it, so tonight I would have to take him at his word.

As I walked slowly downstairs, I remembered my vow not to tell another lie, but this time I felt that they were justified. If I wanted to attend that special church meeting, there was no way I could tell Jerome the truth about the dizzy spell.

Within minutes, Jerome was driving into the church's parking lot. Cars were parked everywhere, and I smiled to myself, thinking that my contacts had come through for me. I looked in Donald's normal parking spot but did not see his white Sentra. Jerome had obviously not been successful in convincing him to come. We found a park in the back of the church and got out and headed for the front. I was relieved to see my siblings waiting outside for me.

Bill was the first to speak. So, what's so important, Tina Mae? Why did you want us to wait out here for you?"

Jerome looked at Bill and then back at me.

"So what's this about?" he asked, sensing that I had not been totally honest with him.

"I have some devastating news I need to share with all of you," I continued. I didn't speak directly to my husband. I needed to speak to my family before heading into the church. I saw the expression on Jerome's face change, indicating his anger, but I simply could not deal with that at the moment.

"Listen, Tina Mae," he said, "you'd better make this quick because I promised Deacon Brown that I would meet with him briefly before the meeting so that he could fill me in on the Deacon's meeting they had earlier."

"Sorry Jerome," I told him, "but what I have to say is far more serious."

Everyone watched in silent anticipation. I didn't want any of the members that were walking by to hear our conversation, so I whispered. "Aunt Minnie called me and said that Rev. White had been blackmailing our father before he died."

Bill looked stunned and seemed to hyperventilate.

"I can't believe this," he was finally able to get out. "Judy called me about an hour ago and told me the same thing. Sarah and I tried to reach you, but you didn't pick up the phone."

It must've been while I was having that dizzy spell. I thought I had heard my house phone ringing, but in that state, I could not be sure.

"Why on earth would Aunt Minnie be calling Judy in Atlanta, Georgia?"

"Judy is not in Atlanta. She was here in town today at a workshop. She didn't want anyone knowing she was staying with Aunt Minnie until after they had had a chance to talk. Sorry I had to keep her secret from you, but I had to do as she asked.

"Everyone knows what's going on besides me?" Rebecca shouted, backing away from the group.

Jerome interrupted. "Don't be upset, Rebecca. That just confirms what I've been telling all of you. That man can't be trusted."

"What are you going to do, Tina Mae?" Bill asked. "You don't think Rev. White will reveal this information at the meeting, do you?"

"Although he promised Aunt Minnie that he would come clean, I don't believe he will. We don't have time for Plan C, so we're going into that church and if Rev. White tries to reveal anything about our father, I'll just have to stop him."

As I walked toward the church steps, I remembered what Aunt Minnie had said about a conversation between Rev. White and Rev. Knighton. I couldn't figure out Rev. Knighton's role in all of this, but I knew I would be able to handle him. I could tell that what had happened had Jerome upset.

"Honey, you still have time to withdraw from this plan," he said. "It appears to me that Rev. White has backed you into a corner. I tried to tell you that he was not trustworthy! That man is dangerous!"

Ignoring Jerome, I turned to my siblings before entering the sanctuary and told them, "We're the McManns, and we stick together. Our plan is to vote Bill in as pastor of Gastonia Church, and our plan will go forward."

I took Jerome's hands into my own and let out a cleansing breath. "This is it!" I told him. "For two years, I've been waiting for this night. Thank you for standing by me all this time." With that said, we walked into the sanctuary to handle our business.

THE VOICE

"You're right," the Voice said. "That is what you had planned for two years. And in a few minutes, your whole life will flash before your eyes. Yes, you're going to witness what actually happened at that meeting."

"What do you mean my whole life will appear before my eyes? It was just a special meeting to elect a pastor at Gastonia Church. But I don't remember if we did."

"Of course you don't. But the pastor you wanted to elected was not Rev. Knighton was it?"

Well, he knows everything anyway, I might as well tell the truth.

"Of course not! It was going to be my brother Bill."

"And whose idea was it to elect your brother Bill?"

"It was my idea. Well – actually, it was my father's idea. He told me to make sure I maintained the legacy of the McMann family. And Bill is the only one who could replace him." "But you kept it a secret. Why?"

"Well, he's a McMann. If he had been ordained before my father passed away, he would have been the next pastor."

"That's not what I asked you, and you know it. You kept it a secret because the Deacon Board nominates a pastor and the members make the final decision. You knew they were going to re-elect Rev. Knighton, but you wanted your brother to be the pastor, so you initiated a secret plan."

"That church belongs to the McMann family, and no one has the right to take it away from us."

"Who do you think is the boss over the churches? The McMann family? The members?"

The Voice seemed agitated with me, but I would not back down.

"My family built that church," I blurted out. "Otherwise, there would not have been a Gastonia Church. No matter what you say, that church belongs to us."

"After you finish reviewing your book of life," the Voice continued, "you will know who the church belongs to."

The Voice paused, so I took the liberty to change the subject.

"So can you tell me why Rev. White blackmailed my father?"

"You are getting ahead of yourself. I will not answer that question just yet. It will be revealed in your book of life."

"How much more time do I have to wait before midnight? I want to know what is happening at the hospital."

"Again you are fast forwarding," the Voice said. "We have not reviewed everything that happened at the special church meeting."

I continued reviewing my book of life. I still had hope. So far, I had not seen anything that would put me on the road to hell, or had I?

CHAPTER THIRTEEN

Walking down the aisle with confidence, I waved to my contacts and smiled. I had instructed them to sit together on the right side of the sanctuary. It would be easier for me to see who was there when it was time to vote. Based on what I observed, the majority of them were present.

Sarah, Rebecca, and I sat on the pew that our father had reserved for the family when he was the pastor. It had been fine sitting that close to the pulpit when my father was alive, but not after Rev. Knighton became the pastor. When he was preaching, I would ignore him and often fall asleep.

One Sunday, I had been snoring so loudly that Sarah had to actually shake my shoulder to wake me up, and forgetting where I was, I let out a loud yawn and stretched, interrupting Rev. Knighton's message. I was a little embarrassed from my behavior, but not enough to go Rev. Knighton to apologize.

I took my seat and reflected on the last special meeting at Gastonia. Most of the members had voted to make Rev. Knighton the pastor of Gastonia Church. Tonight my contacts would reverse that decision. My thought was interrupted when I looked toward the right and saw Rev. Knighton entering the sanctuary. He was dressed in a long white robe, trimmed in gold. Behind him was Deacon Brown dressed in a black suit with a white shirt and black tie, just like Jerome. Suddenly I realized all the deacons were dressed alike.

Deacon Brown must have told Jerome that they were to dress in black and white when he called him about their meeting. And all along, I had thought it was because I had told my family to dress in their best attire. Something was suspicious about all of this!

The meeting was starting in three minutes. Quickly, I reached into my purse and took out my cell phone and texted Bill. Why are all the deacons dressed in black suits? I sat there praying he would hear his cell phone vibrating.

Within seconds, Bill looked at me from where he was sitting in the front on the right side. That area had been reserved for all ministers when there was a special meeting. He hunched his shoulders and raised his eyebrows, indicating that he didn't know.

In the meantime, I touched Sarah and showed her the text I had sent to Bill. "I don't know what Rev. Knighton is trying to pull," I whispered.

I looked to the right and saw Rev. White enter. It was like the devil himself had walked into the sanctuary and sat on the pew with Bill and Rev. Jenkins.

"I'm going to text him," I whispered to Sarah and Rebecca.

Cherice wanted me to be quiet. She shushed me by putting her index finger to her lips, but I just ignored her. After I had revealed Aunt Minnie deep dark secret, she had begged her husband to abandon this plan of ours. "Bill, please let's leave," she begged. "I don't want to be embarrassed here tonight. If you don't come with me, I'll go home alone."

Bill begged her to stay, but we could all tell that she was very uncomfortable with the whole ordeal. The message I texted Rev. White simply said "Blackmail." I knew that would get his attention. He checked his message but did not send a response. Instead, he looked toward where I was sitting for a split second and shifted nervously in his seat.

So, I sent Bill another text. "Tell Rev. White that I've talked to Aunt Minnie."

Bill read my message and turned toward Rev. White, lightly tapped him on the shoulder, and whispered in his ear.

Rev. White's reaction was not what I expected. He had the saddest expression I could ever have imagined. It appeared that he might cry any minute. As he leaned over to respond to Bill, Rev. Knighton rose to call the meeting to order. Rev. Knighton asked everyone to bow as he offered a word of prayer. I only recall his ending words. "Lord, please let what takes place here tonight let it be in Your best interest. We yield this prayer to You. Amen."

In unison, everyone said, "Amen."

What was going to take place other than the election? I sat up in my seat and tried to focus, but I was worried. Knowing that Rev. White was a blackmailer and seeing the Deacons dressed in their communion attire made me a little leery, but I had to appear confident.

Suddenly, it dawned on me. Communion was served on the fourth Friday in May at our regular meeting, so maybe that was for reason for the Deacons to be dressed in their uniform black and white. Maybe they had decided to do it the second Friday instead. But then again, my rationale didn't make sense because my husband surely would have told me about the change. No, something about this was amiss.

As Rev. Knighton continued, the side door opened and a White minister who appeared to be in his late fifties entered the sanctuary. He was dressed like Rev. Knighton and carried a black Bible in one hand and a brown book in the other. He nodded to Rev. Knighton and took a seat near the other ministers.

The members seemed awestruck. A White person in the sanctuary of our church was certainly an anomaly. My contacts look directly at me with questioning eyes. "Who is that White Man? And why is he here?" Of course I didn't know the answer, but I was not about to let them know that I didn't have everything under control. I pretended to know what was happening by giving them a confident nod. But at the same time I was confused. I had no idea what was about to happen. But whatever it was would not sabotage my plan. I simply wouldn't allow it.

Rev. Knighton continued, looking directly at me. "I know some of you didn't agree with remodeling the sanctuary, but all repairs have been completed. Deacon Brown has done a fantastic job of minimizing the costs and keeping us well under budget. Deacons, I praise God for you. You have worked hard supporting the various ministries and assuring that our church reaches the standard of excellence that is sure to please our God."

I sat there trying to control my emotions, but I wanted to yell, "Enough already!" Yes, I had been against the renovations, but my concern at this meeting was the election only. Anything else, in my opinion, was a waste of time.

"I was amazed," he continued, "when I saw so many members here tonight. Some of you, I don't recognize, but I'm sure you're members otherwise you wouldn't be here." With that, he chuckled.

My mind went directly to our White visitor. He was certainly not a member, so what was he doing at the meeting?

At that moment, a member stood abruptly and said, "Can we just get on with the election? I thought all I had to do was come the church and vote and go home. I don't mean to be disrespectable, but I've got things to do!"

I turned slightly and realized that the person speaking was one of my contacts, Angelina. I bowed my head and whispered a prayer. "Lord, please don't let me be embarrassed by Angelina's actions tonight. Help her to calm down and exercise self-restraint. Amen."

I understood Angelina's behavior. Her mother had passed away eight years ago. Being the only child with no other close family members, she had not been able to deal with her loss. Instead of giving her life to Christ, she had become an alcoholic.

Rev. Knighton, looked at her and said in a serious tone. "I'm sorry sister, but you're out of order. Remember, this is the Lord's house and we want to conduct ourselves in a Christian manner. We won't be long, I promise you."

I looked at Angelina and motioned for her to be quiet. She turned around in her seat and smacked her lips. I was really worried about what she might do or say next. After all, she was obviously intoxicated and not functioning rationally. But I needed her to get herself together. After all, I had given her more money than I had given anyone else. She had been late on her house payment and car payment, so of course I had helped her out. It had been hard getting her to come to the meeting in the first place. I just prayed that she would not bolt before the election.

I focused my attention back on Rev. Knighton, thinking the election was about to begin. But I was wrong. Rev. Knighton explained the order of the meeting had been changed. The Deacon Board had granted him permission to perform an ordination service before the election. I looked at my husband and then at my siblings. Just like the other members, we were amazed. I had messed up everything by calling that emergency meeting earlier. Had it not been for that meeting, Jerome would have known what was going on.

I began panicking. It became crystal clear to me why Rev. Knighton had not wanted me to have an agenda. But I was still determined. My plan would go forth, no matter what.

Without hesitation, I jumped up to speak. Everyone was watching. I glanced at Jerome and read his expression that said, "I told you couldn't pull this off." Bill's expression was one of defeat, and Sarah directed her focus toward the front of the sanctuary nervously shaking her legs and acting as if I were a perfect stranger. But Rebecca was in my corner. She glared at Rev. Knighton with apparent anger.

Rev. Knighton paused and then he looked directly at me. “Sister Tina Mae, would you like to speak? Because you know you’re out of order,” he said with an even tone.

Knowing everyone was watching, I cleared my throat. “Did I understand correctly that the election will be held after the ordination service?” I asked in a tone that expressed my displeasure.

“Yes,” he replied, “that’s correct, Sister Tina. “So now may we continue? Like I said, you’re out of order.”

Rev. Knighton, I said, “I want to set the record straight. According to the church by-laws, election is to be held every two years the second Friday in May, but it doesn’t say anything about an ordination service on that night. If there were going to be any changes, shouldn’t the Deacons agree before they can be made?”

Rev. Knighton was speaking in slow motion, “Sister-Tina - Mae, you must have not been listening because I already said the Deacon Board had agreed. They approved the changes at their meeting this afternoon.”

I stood there for a moment speechless, while the entire congregation was silent. I kept repeating to myself under my breath, "He can't win." There I was thinking Rev. White was going to embarrass the McMann family, but it was Rev. Knighton instead. I knew he had been planning something, but not to that magnitude.

I stood there for a few seconds, and then Rev. Knighton asked, "Are you finished?" When I was able to collect my thoughts, I responded.

"If it's not in the bylaws to have an ordination service on an election night, why is it necessary?"

Rev. Knighton's tone changed. "I don't have to go by the by-laws, Sister Tina Mae. I go by the One who is in control of all of us. If I consult with Him and then get approval of the Deacons, that's all that's necessary. Even though you don't understand now, you will soon!"

He might as well have slapped me in the face. That was not the answer I wanted to hear. I was demanding. "Why it is so important to ordain the Deacons in training tonight? They were just appointed six months ago. We could do that at another time!"

Rev. Knighton didn't answer my question. He just said, "Sister Tina Mae, we can't be here all night, please have a seat so that we can continue."

I didn't know whether to take my seat or just blurt out my secret plan right then and there. I decided that to calm down and take my seat might be best.

Feeling that he had "won," Rev. Knighton smiled. He then asked all of the Ministers and Deacons to come to the altar and face the congregation.

"Tonight, I want to reveal to you a secret that I have kept with Deacon Brown for the past two years," he said.

My heart was pounding so loudly that to me it sounded like a full drum line of a college band. I could not believe that Rev. Knighton was actually going to come clean about the homosexual relationship he had shared with Deacon Brown.

But wait a minute! Maybe the White minister was there to perform their wedding before the ordination service. No way were the members going to have a gay minister as a pastor. I chuckled at the thought.

What Rev. Knighton said next completely wiped the smile off of my face. He told the members that Deacon Brown was going to be ordained. "For the past two years," he told them, "Deacon Brown has been in seminary studying to become a minister. He signed his license Friday."

Bill and I looked at each other. I'm sure we thought alike. Rev. Knighton was going to appoint Deacon Brown as the assistant pastor. He had no intention of appointing Bill.

Well, that just meant that Bill would have to put up with Deacon Brown as his assistant for two years, and then he would be able to appoint whomever he chose as his assistant. I just hoped Bill would be able to tolerate Deacon Brown that long.

Rev. Knighton and the White preacher, who I later learned was Rev. Neil, performed the ordination service. When Rev. Knighton pronounced Deacon Brown as one of the ministers of Gastonia church, he grinned from ear to ear. To my surprise, the members didn't reject.

Everyone was on their feet applauding, even my contacts. Watching what was going on, I was displeased to say the least. Then it dawned on me that the Rev. Brown, now a minister, could no longer serve as Chairman of the Deacon Board. My mind went into overdrive.

Once Bill became the pastor, he would be sure to appoint my Jerome to replace him. Everything was working in our favor. All I had to do was nominate Bill for pastor and let the vote take place.

Rev. Knighton thanked Rev. Neil for assisting him with the ordination service and then he left the sanctuary, waving goodbye to the members. I closed my eyes briefly and envisioned my family back in control of Gastonia Church. I loved what was about to take place. It was finally happening.

CHAPTER FOURTEEN

Rev. Brown remained at the altar to speak to the members. He stared at me with an expression of victory, feeling that he had won the battle. But little did he know that I was still holding the ace card, and I would win the war after I revealed my secret plan.

"I'd like to thank all of you for accepting me as a minister of Gastonia Church. A burden has been lifted off my shoulders. I promise I will not disappoint you."

With that vote of thanks, we all thought that he was about to take his seat, but he had yet another surprise. Looking in my direction, he said to a young lady a few pews behind me "Stand up, baby."

Of course, I turned around in my seat to look in the direction he was pointing. Standing three pews behind me dressed in a pink pantsuit was Jennifer Jenkins. I nearly passed out. His "baby" was none other than the daughter of two of my best friends, Catherine and her husband, Rev. Ralph Jenkins.

"Jennifer and I attended seminary together," he continued, "and we've formed a close relationship. After graduation, I proposed to her on her birthday. Our wedding will be held here at Gastonia Church within the next nine months. You're all invited."

The members all stared in amazement. I was dumbfounded and speechless. I needed a glass of water because I felt that my body temperature had risen one hundred degrees. Jennifer just stood there with pride. Brushing her long black weave across her shoulder and flashing a big diamond on her finger. I felt like a tractor-trailer truck had just hit me. It became clear to me why Catherine had been acting strangely in the doctor's office; she had been withholding her daughter's secret. She couldn't tell me because she knew that I didn't like Rev. Brown because he had replaced my husband, Jerome as chairman of the Deacon Board. It was apparent that Catherine and Rev. Jenkins were going to stand by their daughter. That's why they had withdrawn from our secret plan. I wondered if that was the reason the other ministers had withdrawn as well.

But I had to focus on what was important at the moment, making sure that my brother was elected Pastor. I couldn't let Rev. Brown's revelation cause me to lose sight of my goal. I had to stay focused. I knew my contacts would be watching me to see how I would handle the situation. I had to be cool and not show that my confidence was shaken. It was bad enough that I had led them to believe that Rev. Knighton and the now Rev. Brown were homosexuals.

Boy, had I blown that one! I bowed my head and prayed that my contacts would not hold that against me and would still vote with the McMann family as they had promised. So, I was wrong about them! They had spent so much time together that anyone would have made the same assumption. Even though Rev. Brown's disclosure had made me look like an idiot, I still felt that I had the upper hand.

Because Rev. Brown was no longer a Deacon, he called the co-chair, Deacon Murphy forward to proceed with the election. I whispered to Sarah, "Rev. Knighton has known all along that he was going to appoint Rev. Brown to be the assistant pastor."

She nodded but didn't say anything.

Deacon Murphy stood at the podium, gripping it tightly. It was obvious that he was extremely nervous.

"This is the first time I've presided over a special meeting," he said clearing his throat a couple of times, "so please bear with me. I'm a little nervous."

He took a white handkerchief from inside his jacket and wiped his face and then reached for his reading glasses. Rev. Brown saw that he was struggling, so he walked to the podium and handed him a slip of paper. I was sure it was instructions on how to proceed. Deacon Murphy nodded his appreciation and continued.

It was annoying not having an agenda. I didn't know what direction the meeting was going. I felt that time was running out. Glancing at my husband and then my siblings, I stood to speak. Deacon Murphy saw me because our eyes met, but instead of giving me the floor, he asked Rev. Knighton to speak. Our normal protocol was that the pastor in line for re-election, didn't speak until after he had been voted back into that position. I knew something was up, so I eased down in my seat, curious to see what would happen next.

Deacon Murphy continued. "Rev. Knighton, please share with the congregation what we discussed in our meeting earlier. Deacon Black was not able to attend, but the rest of us are in agreement with your proposal."

I looked at Jerome and then at my siblings. It appeared that the ordination of Rev. Brown would not be the only secret revealed this evening. But if I had my way, Rev. Knighton would not be getting away with another "trick."

Rev. Knighton stood and faced the congregation. He reached under the podium for a tissue, and that is when I realized that tears were rolling down his face. Then he began to speak, with his voice quivering. "I know you are here to re-elect me as pastor," he said. "Well, some of you. For the last two years, it has been a joy to have served you."

I didn't know where he was going with this, so my stomach was in knots and my head pounding. Then he continued.

"I stand here this evening to announce that I will be withdrawing my name from the election. I informed the

Deacons earlier of my decision. When I arrived at Gastonia Church, it was in turmoil."

When he said that, I was furious. How could he belittle my father that way? But I sat quietly as he continued.

"But with the help of God, a wonderful group of Deacons, and all of you, we've been able to turn things around and put this church back to what God intended it to be. The membership had increased from seventy-five members to five hundred. And we are finally focusing on the Spiritual rather than merely the physical. I've finished my course here. I've done what God has asked me to do, so now I'll be moving on. I will certainly keep in touch because you are like family to me, but tonight, I have to bid you farewell."

The members were silent for about three minutes. When I looked around, tears were flowing freely from the eyes of just about everyone, even my contacts. I sat there blown away. My siblings were looking at me wanting to know what I was going to do. My mind was already calculating my next move. If he was not going to be the pastor, then who was?

My thoughts were cluttered. I had to come up with another plan. My mind was running a mile a minute. I didn't know what to do. My two years had been for naught. I wondered if Rev. White had told Rev. Knighton about our secret plan and if that knowledge had in some way influenced his decision to resign. I was elated that he was resigning, but still a little disappointed that I would not get to see the expression of shock on his face when I stood to nominate my brother to run against him. But the main objective was to get Bill elected, and now, with the pastor position vacated, my task would be quite easy.

CHAPTER FIFTEEN

As I struggled to compose myself, Rev. Knighton looked away from the congregation toward the Deacons. "Before I depart, I want you to know that I will not leave the church without able leadership," he said, still overcome with emotion. "The Deacons and I have agreed on the person they will be nominating to replace me."

I held back from screaming. How could the Deacons allow a resigning pastor to have any say in his replacement? I would not let them get away with this. And I would not blame myself for asking Jerome to be at my emergency meeting rather than his Deacon's meeting. Rev. Brown had ample time to contact Jerome and let him know what had been decided. I knew that this had all been a plan to keep my family and me in the dark. And I was not about to let them get away with it. As I sat there getting more and more angrily, I soon remembered that I actually still had the upper hand. I had enough contacts there to override any decision of the Deacon Board. Why was I worried?

I glanced over at Jerome and saw him whisper something to Deacon Parker. He nodded and then looked over at me with an expression of shock. His face told me that he felt that I should abandon our plan, but I shook my head and formed the words "No way" on my lips. My secret plan was not going to turn into a disaster. Rev. Knighton had released the last trick up his sleeve. I was not worried. I had two hundred contacts to support me and my brother was going to be the pastor of Gastonia Church.

Rev. Knighton chose not to reveal the name of his replacement. Instead, he walked toward the door as the congregation stood to give him a standing ovation.

When everyone took their seats, Deacon Murphy continued.

"Tina Mae before I let you speak, I will reveal the decision of the Deacon Board."

I could tell that his nervousness was about to get the best of him. He was sweating profusely and his hands shook uncontrollably.

"Gastonia Church needs a pastor that can help us grow, and the deacons have voted unanimously to appoint Rev. Brown." Then he entertained a motion.

I was mortified. So, that was why Rev. Knighton had thrown protocol to the wind and ordained Rev. Brown at the meeting earlier. The motion was on the floor to accept Rev. Brown's nomination, but before anyone could second it, I stood to speak.

"Deacon Murphy, I know there is no written agenda, and I hope I'm not out of order, but I have something to say. First of all, who ever heard of a resigning pastor naming his replacement? I stand to nominate my brother Bill McMann, Jr. as pastor of Gastonia Church."

"Tina Mae, you are out of order," Deacon Murphy said, appearing to gain some confidence. "The board has made their decision and that's final. If you wanted to nominate another candidate, you should have submitted the name to the Deacon Board for consideration. Your husband knows the rules. Did he know you were planning to nominate your brother?"

"Of course he knows the rules, but the members have the last say." I looked around at my contacts, hoping they would have my back. Huh. Their blank expressions revealed that they were not quite sure what was happening. But I was not giving up.

"All these members here tonight," I said, pointing to my contacts, "are not here in support of Rev. Knighton. They're here to support the McMann family, and they want to elect Bill as pastor of Gastonia Church."

Deacon Murphy took a step back away from the podium and turned his attention to the Deacon for their support. He glanced over at my contacts and then back to the Deacons. Then he lashed out at Jerome.

"Deacon Black, I'm surprised at you," he spat out. "You knew your wife was planning to vote out Rev. Knighton tonight and nominate your brother-in-law. Why didn't you tell her to follow protocol? Oh, let me guess. She told you not to tell and of course you do everything she tells you to do!"

The anger in his voice was obvious. Before my husband could speak, I jumped to his defense.

"Well, the members didn't know about the ordination service, and that's not how things are supposed to be done. How dare you nominate Rev. Brown, and he was just was ordained tonight! He doesn't have any experience! My brother has been ordained for two years!"

"Tina Mae, the Deacon Board decides who they want to present to the members. Rev. McMann's name was not given to us for consideration, and we're not going to bend the rules."

I wasn't about to let it go, so I continued to press. But there were other ministers here who've been ordained for years. Why weren't they considered?"

"At our meeting, Rev. Brown told us he was going to be ordained tonight and that Rev. Knighton would be resigning. We knew we needed to act right away, and with all due respect, the board felt that Rev. Brown would be the best candidate. With much prayer, he will lead Gastonia Church in the right direction."

"But this is a democracy," I protested. "The congregation should have their say in the matter, and I say that we take a vote!"

I was really going out on a limb. I was not certain that my contacts would understand how I intended for them to vote. Maybe they thought that my main goal was to get rid of Rev. Knighton, and since he was gone, then they could vote however they wished. But I had to take that chance.

Deacon Murphy was persistent in his decision. “Tina Mae, please be seated,” he said. “I will not let this meeting get out of hand. We are a spiritual body, and I intend for us to be led by the spirit in all that we do here this evening!”

I have had quite enough. I was not going to allow Deacon Murphy to speak to me that way, so I walked to the front of the sanctuary and turned to face the members.

“I don’t approve of the decision of the Deacons,” I said. “Tonight, I'm here to nominate my brother Bill, as pastor of Gastonia Church!”

The members, including my family all sat there astonished. No one dared to say a word, and that is when it began happening.

I seemed to be losing my vision. I tried to speak but found that I could not form my words. I felt my legs giving way, so I steadied myself by holding onto the podium. I knew that my getting upset had triggered another dizzy spell.

Then Judy came and stood next to me at the podium. For a brief moment, I thought that she had come because she had sensed that I was in trouble, but when she spoke, I knew I had been mistaken.

"Deacon Murphy, I'm sorry I have to interrupt this meeting," she said, pushing me aside with no regard for my obvious medical emergency. "But my sister is about to make the biggest mistake of her life."

As if he had not truly heard what Judy had said, Deacon Murphy continued.

"What in the world is going on with you McManns? Have you come here just to cause a disturbance this evening? We will have order in this meeting! This is the Lord's house!"

"Deacon Murphy, I understand that, and I've come for peace," Judy said. "It's not what you think. I'm here to prevent my brother from becoming the pastor. I'm here to stop my sister from making the biggest mistake of her life," she repeated. "Please, may I speak?"

Deacon Murphy looked toward the Deacons for their nod of approval since he knew that Judy was out of order. The deacons nodded to let her speak.

I stood there, trying to gain my composure and wondering what on earth Judy was about to say. I glanced over at my other siblings and realized that they were as much in the dark about what Judy was about to say. It was then that I knew without a shadow of a doubt that I had to stop her.

Judy cleared her throat and then grabbed my hand and looked me straight in the eye, with tears welling up in her eyes.

"Tina Mae, I have to do this," she said wiping the tears that had begun to spill down her cheeks. I stood closer to the podium for support. I didn't want to fall.

"Even though you might not believe me," she continued, "I love you dearly. You're my sister. I just want to protect you. The truth must be told before you regret what you are about to do."

I saw my two years of planning turning into a disaster. Rev. Knighton had done enough damage. I didn't want to hear any more surprises. I was being attacked, and no one was there to help me.

If Judy didn't speak quickly, I didn't know how much longer I would be able to use the podium to support myself. My legs were wobbling again, and I could barely see Judy standing beside me. But I tried to stay focused as much as I could.

Judy released my hands and then turned facing the members and said, "I'm here to put an end to my sister's secret plan," she said sadly.

Deacon Murphy could not conceal his surprise. He looked directly at Jerome. "Deacon Black, do you know anything about this secret plan? Does it have anything to do with this election?" he asked, thinking that Jerome would be loyal to his position as Deacon.

But before Jerome could respond, Judy spoke up. "I think Rev. White can explain," she said.

Rev. White rose from his seat. I cannot say whether he rose to leave or to address the congregation, but Bill pulled him back down and told him in a tone loud enough for those seated near them to hear, "You need to apologize to the church for blackmailing my father!"

It only took a few seconds for the whispering to take over the atmosphere. "Blackmail? Who's been blackmailed? Was it Rev. Knighton? Is that why he left?"

As is normally the case, a whisper had been heard and it had taken on a life of its own. The meeting truly was getting out of hand.

It was Judy who tried to regain control. "Please everyone, I can explain," she said. "My Aunt Minnie had access to some of my father's important records after he passed away. While at her house this afternoon, I searched through those files and discovered that my father and Rev. White had a deep dark secret. This will explain everything."

That is when I saw the envelope in her hand. She handed it to me. "You can decide whether or not you want to read it aloud," she said.

I refused to read it. Well actually I couldn't read it. My vision was so blurred that I wouldn't be able to see anything clearly. I heard myself say weakly, "I just want to elect Bill as the pastor of this church. I've got to fulfill my father's request."

Suddenly, I was gasping for breath and felt darkness encompass me. I sensed that I was falling to the floor. I couldn't move, but I could still hear voices.

CHAPTER SIXTEEN

"I can't take this anymore," I said to The Voice. "Can you just tell me why I'm here?"

"Just continue viewing," the Voice demanded. But I didn't want to continue. I was not prepared to hear any negativity against my father. Realizing that I had no say in the matter, I did as I was told and went back to my Book of Life.

I was still at the special church meeting, and my dizziness has subsided somewhat. Judy was presenting the canceled checks that our father had written to Rev. White. She was amazed that Rev. White had been blackmailing our father.

I knew my father hadn't dotted every "I" or crossed every "T," but I thought he had been an honorable man. I was somewhat relieved to find out that the $100,000 had been paid to Rev. White under duress and that my father had not spent the money for personal gain.

"Turn toward the road!" he said, "And don't say another word! Someone will speak with you shortly.
I looked around, with my eyes widening, but I didn't see anyone. I wanted to speak, but I was told not to. Who could be on that road other than the devil?"

A strange sound interrupted my thought. It was a faint voice, one that was eerily familiar. When I listened more intently, I realized that it was my father's voice. I didn't know how I was supposed to feel. If I were on my way to Hell, I certainly didn't want to see my father here, but it was certainly wonderful to hear a familiar sound. I heard the voice, but I had yet to see him.

My mind went back to the days when he used to play Hide and Seek with me. I remembered one day in particular when he had been playing with me when he received an important phone call and had gone inside, forgetting to come and find me. My mother saw me standing behind the large oak tree from the kitchen window, waiting patiently for my father. Knowing he had forgotten me, she opened the door and told me to come inside. It broke my heart that he had forgotten me, but I forgave him nonetheless. I just hoped he would be able to help shed some light as to why I was in this place and would not leave me here alone, like he had done all those years earlier.

Without hesitation, I cried out, "Father, is that you?"

It was the Voice, not my father that responded. "Yes, that's your father," he said. "I brought him here to explain firsthand what Judy was trying to reveal to you."

"Daddy, this is Tina Mae," I said to him. "The Voice brought you here to explain what Judy was saying about you. Is it true you that Rev. White blackmailed you? Is that why you're on this road, for taking money from the church?"

"Tina Mae, I will explain later. There's something you need to know before I tell you about the blackmailing."

"So it is true?"

"Tina Mae, I know about your secret plan. The Voice told me everything. The reason Judy didn't want you to fulfill my request is because..."

"Because you and she never got along," I interrupted.

"You two couldn't see eye to eye on anything." Tears were now streaming down my face. "I'm sorry I didn't fulfill your request, Daddy. I know I've disappointed the McMann family."

"Tina Mae, you don't have to be sorry. It's not your fault. You don't have to worry about that anymore. The Voice bought me here to explain that Judy told the truth. Rev. White was blackmailing me. Unfortunately, you will have to bear the consequences of what I've done."

Suddenly my tears subsided, and I felt anger creep in. I could not believe what he was saying.

"But why, Daddy? What have you gotten me into? I trusted you. All that work I put into trying to execute a plan to comply with your wishes, and you're now saying it was all for naught? You've set me up just like you did Aunt Minnie. Now, because of you, I'm facing going on that road to Hell with you. Hell is not my home. I'm not going there because of you!"

"Listen to me, Tina Mae. I don't want you to join me on this road to Hell," he explained. "I deceived everyone, including you. But it's too late for me to ask for forgiveness, but I've got to make this right with you."

My father was silent for what seemed like a long time, and then he continued. "Listen, my child, there was a secret that your mother and I carried with us to our graves."

"What kind of secret?" I asked hesitantly.

"Please try to understand. We thought we were protecting you. But it's now time for you to know the whole truth. Rev. White is your biological father."

I could not believe what I was hearing. And my "father" had said it so matter-of-factly, just as he might say that the sky is blue. I started to hyperventilate and reached for my chest, as if I could steady my now irregular heartbeat.

"My biological father?" I repeated. "But that can't be. You're not my father. Are you saying that you've arranged for me to come here to this place just so you shatter my world with this? How could you and my mother do this to me?"

My mind went back to the envelope that Judy had handed to me the night of the church meeting. I thought back to her words, "Read this aloud if you want to." Now everything was clear. The letter she had given to me contained this awful revelation. I wondered if she had informed the congregation after my blackout.

"Tina Mae, it's a long story. Please try to understand," the man I thought was my father continued to plead.

"What's there to understand? You were very clear. You just told me that Rev. White is my father."

My life had changed in a matter of seconds. I fell to my knees and sobbed for a long time. By withholding this truth, my father had put me in an awkward position. In an effort to uphold his legacy, I had made many enemies. My behavior had been shameful, and if I was allowed to go back, I would be humiliated.

I thought back to how I had treated Rev. Knighton. I had made it virtually impossible for him to do his job. I deserved to go to Hell, right along with my father. And there was nothing he could do to save me.

Then I remembered Aunt Minnie warning me not to trust Rev. White. I wished I had listened, but he had led me to believe that he was my friend. And what Jerome had perceived as flirting was actually Rev. White's way of getting close to me to form a relationship.

This was all so sick! My "father" continued to speak. He explained that my mother and Rev. White had been high school sweethearts until he went into the army. During the time while he was home on leave, I had been conceived. Rev. White had refused to face up to his responsibility, so my "father" married my mother, adopted me, and raised me as his very own. Everything had worked just fine until I turned six. At that time, Rev. White had had a change of heart and wanted to visit me, so of course they agreed. He brought gifts that day, and they never stopped until the day I graduated from college.

I always wondered why I had gotten a bike, my own TV, and so many other nice things that my siblings didn't have. I thought it was just because I was the oldest.

"Enough of that," I said. "Just tell me why Rev. White was blackmailing you.

He paused and then continued. "The year your mother passed away, Rev. White had threatened to reveal the secret if she did not agree to pay him huge sums of money, but she died before he could follow through. I knew he was in a financial bind, but his behavior was inexcusable. After your mother's death, I thought he would drop it, but that didn't happen. He started in on me, demanding that I pay him monthly to keep quiet. He knew how important you were to me and how much I wanted to protect the legacy of Gastonia Church, so he figured I would comply, and comply I did. That's when the payments started. And they continued until your Aunt Minnie figured everything out and refused to continue to write the checks for me."

By then, my "father" had paid Rev. White well over $100,000, which he had intended to pay back to the church. But he had not anticipated getting sick or a decline in the membership of Gastonia Church. The stress of it all had added to his early demise.

After listening to my father's confession, I somehow felt a sense of relief. I was at this place, in danger of the fires of Hell because of him and Rev. White. Now that he had told me the truth, there was no reason for me to go to Hell. Even The Voice would understand that what I had done was honorable because I was carrying out his request.

Lost in my thoughts, I heard my "father" say, "Tina Mae, my time is up. I have to go now, but whatever you do, please don't come on this road with me. I am sorry that you were enticed by my requests to do bad things."

“Make no mistake about it,” I told him. “There's no way I’m going on that road with you. I hate it for you, but you're on your own!”

Suddenly, my “father” was gone and everything was silent, that is except for his words echoing in my head, “Don't come down this road!”

I pondered. Knowing that my actions had been prompted by a deception, I felt that my actions would be forgiven. Rev. White was a part of his sin. He should be the one facing the road to Hell.

Just when I thought I was going to be beamed back to my reality, the Voice shocked me again. “Not so fast,” he demanded. “You have sins that you must give an account of!”

“But I haven’t blackmailed anyone!” I protested. “What other sins am I guilty of?” The Voice did not answer me. He simply motioned me back to the Book of Life and asked me to view what was happening at the hospital. I complied out of desperation. What else could I do?

CHAPTER SEVENTEEN

The stress of viewing my Book of Life for hours along with communicating with my father had been mentally exhausting. I just wanted all of this to be over.

Suddenly, I remembered that I had been given until midnight to regain consciousness. If not, Doctor Ellis would have a specialist to re-evaluate my condition. That explained why The Voice had told me to view what was going on at the hospital. I walked closer to the Golden Gate. Bowing my head I murmured, "I wouldn't be in the hospital if I had abided by Doctor Ellis's order."

The Voice responded, "You wouldn't be in the hospital if you had just heeded those warnings."

"What warnings?" I asked innocently.

"Three times you were warned to drop your secret plan. Because of your overly tenacious attitude, you just ignored them. Your main focus was Rev. Knighton. It was disgraceful how you meddled with him and refused to allow him to finish the work God had called him to do at Gastonia Church."

How was I supposed to know that I should have taken those warnings seriously? Yes, my high blood pressure should have gotten my attention. And if not that, then certainly the dizzy spells, but they had only landed me in the hospital. Why was my body there and my spirit here?

I just stood there staring at Doctor Ellis talking to my family and giving instructions to my nurse. I tried to yell, "Help me," but who was I kidding? No one could help me. I had to continue fighting on my own to return to my family.

Doctor Ellis glanced toward the huge clock on the wall. It was 11:52 p.m.

"If she doesn't regain consciousness in the next eight minutes," he said, "it's unlikely that she will be able to make a full recovery. She's been unconscious way too long. If I were you, I'd pray!"

"What's going to happen if I don't regain consciousness?" I asked The Voice, barely able to maintain my composure.

"You're fast forwarding again," he said. "The answers to all your questions are in your Book of Life. Just continue viewing."

In spite of what I had done, I still hoped that I would survive. I simply couldn't give up. I looked back into my book. I was still in the hospital bed, and my husband and daughter were sitting in the same area. From their disheveled clothing, it appeared that they had been there for quite some time.

I felt empathy seeing my daughter sitting there holding my hands, watching the minutes tick away, and whispering in my ear, "Please, Mom, wake up." I could sense that she was losing hope. Then I saw Bill enter. I would have understood had chosen not to come to the hospital to see me. I had caused him such anguish in forcing him to agree to become pastor of Gastonia Church, knowing all the time that he was only going along with my wishes.

As I continued to survey the room, I saw Rebecca and Sarah sitting at the foot of my bed. I felt confident that they would forgive me for the pain I had caused the family. Judy held the Bible and looked intently at the clock. It was about five minutes before midnight when she asked everyone to form a circle. Then she began to pray. I knew then without a shadow of a doubt that my little sister truly loved me.

Dr. Ellis walked over to the nurse and whispered into her ear. She nodded, and they both glanced at the clock. Stepping away from viewing my book of life, I turned toward The Voice. “I have only two minutes to wake up,” I told him. “Can you just tell me what's going to happen? I don’t want to look anymore.”

“Open your eyes,” The Voice said, for the first time in a soft tone. “I'm going to give you a second chance. You’re going to regain consciousness.”

“You mean I’m going back to my family and not down that road to Hell?” I asked excitedly.

“You will regain consciousness by midnight, but you will have a major assignment to fulfill,” he said. “If you don't comply, I will bring you back here and you will go down that dreaded road!”

His voice was not angry, but I knew he meant what he had said. He told me that my assignment, which was to be completed within the next twenty-four hours, was to ask Rev. Knighton and the members of Gastonia Church to forgive me for my wrongdoings.

At first, I protested. "How on earth will I be able to accomplish that?" I argued. "I have no idea where Rev. Knighton is, and the church has almost 500 members! That's impossible!"

"It's not impossible," The Voice told me still in an even tone. "There will be a church gathering tomorrow at 4:00 p.m. When you collapsed at the special meeting, Deacon Murphy adjourned and asked the members to come back tomorrow at 4:00 so that Rev. Brown's appointment as Pastor could be made official."

"But will Rev. Knighton be there? He's the most important person I need to speak with."

"It will be your responsibility to make the necessary contacts to make sure he is there. If you value your soul, make it happen!"

The thought of being reunited with my family, especially my daughter and husband overwhelmed me. And then I heard the clock strike midnight, and magically I was in my hospital room, struggling to lift my head off the pillow. I could not, but was able to squeeze my husband's hand.

"Dr. Ellis, she just squeezed my hand," he said excitedly. "She knows we're here!"

Dr. Ellis joined my husband at my bedside and checked my blood pressure. I was told that it had been extremely high when I got to the hospital, but now it was normal. Dr. Ellis checked my other vitals and reported that they were all normal. I sat up in my hospital bed and looked around in a daze. Tears welled in my eyes and I began to thank God aloud for sparing my life and giving me such a supportive family.

My husband was overjoyed and my daughter reached down and gave me a big hug. Everyone began speaking at once, trying to explain to me what had happened. Although I already knew from having observed my "Book of Life," I just let them speak. Clearly, I couldn't explain to them what I had encountered. My current focus was on fulfilling the assignment that The Voice had given me, and time was of the essence.

"Dr. Ellis thanks so much for everything, but can I please go home now," I begged.

"She's back to normal, everybody," Jerome laughed. "She hates for people to make a fuss over her.

"Go home?" Dr. Ellis said, raising his eyebrows and ignoring the laughter in the room. "Well it certainly won't be tonight. If you continue improving, and all your tests come back okay, then I'll discharge you in the morning. I don't see any reason why I should keep you here."

That was good news to my ears. I wanted to begin my task as soon as possible. Lisa and Jerome were so relieved that they refused to leave my side.

They stayed with me at the hospital all night. The next morning Dr. Ellis discharged me just as he had promised.

CHAPTER EIGHTEEN

When I reached my own house, my anxiety relief replaced my relief. I had to figure out a way to convince my husband to allow me to attend a church meeting on the same day of my release from the hospital. I knew it would not be easy, especially since the stress of the special church meeting was in his mind, what had landed me there in the first place. He had demanded that I go directly to our bedroom to relax. When he came in to check on me, I figured that was the time to work my charm.

"Honey," I started in my most loving voice, "I know you probably won't think this is a good idea, but do you think I could accompany you to the special meeting at church this afternoon?"

"And how did you know about that meeting?" he asked startled. Then I remembered that neither he nor my daughter had told me. The Voice had given me that information.

"Oh, I thought I overheard Judy or Sarah or someone mention it yesterday evening just before leaving the hospital," I lied.

"Tina Mae, I really don't think it is a good idea to expose yourself to stress right now. Don't you think you should take it easy a few days?"

"But you don't understand, Honey," I begged. "I've got to go. I want to; I need to apologize to the congregation for my behavior of the past two years." His concern was replaced with shock, but pleasant shock.

"I'm so proud of you, baby. Apologizing is the Christian thing to do."

With that, he sat down on the bed beside me and stared into my eyes.

"I really believe you are doing the right thing. This will be good for you and for your entire family. And believe it or not, the Deacons met earlier today to decide my fate in helping you with your plan to elect your brother. They have decided to forgive me. Deacon Murphy called earlier to give me the good news. God is so awesome!"

Staring deeply into my eyes, he said, “I’m amazed you are not going to pursue your secret plan...”

Lisa interrupted our conversation when she entered with my lunch on a tray. I was starving for a home cooked meal, since it had been hours since I’d eaten. Ravenously, I ate the casserole and bread she had prepared and then drank the ice tea. I loved the fact that Lisa was taking care of me, and I didn't want her attentiveness to end. It had been two years since the two of us had communicated, and I had no desire to mess this up.

“Here I am, worrying about what to say to the members,” I thought to myself, “when I haven't even apologized to my own daughter.”

With that thought, I got up from my bed and took her hands into mine. “Lisa, I want to apologize to you,” I said with all the sincerity I could muster.” I put maintaining my father's legacy before you, and I am asking for your forgiveness. I know I've been impossible for the past two years, and I just want you to know that I will spend what's left of my life making it up to you. “

Lisa held my hands tighter. “It's okay, Mom,” she said. “It's just great to have you back.” “Back for now,” I thought, “unless I get that assignment done.”

Jerome followed Lisa downstairs to have lunch with her. Silence was exactly what I needed. I had to figure out a way to contact Rev. Knighton. I felt confident that Rev. Brown would be able to get in touch with him, so I reached for my cell phone. I stared at it for a few seconds and then decided that I must be kidding myself. No way was I about to call Rev. Brown, not after what I had done at the special meeting. He would probably refuse to talk to me. But I had to stay strong. With or without his help, I would contact Rev. Knighton and apologize. And I would let the entire membership know how sorry I was for my inexcusable behavior.

In a few hours, that burden of sin and guilt would be removed from me, and I would be allowed to remain with my family and be on my right road finally, the one to Heaven.

* * * *

When I entered inside the sanctuary, I could tell that the members were shocked to see me there. I looked straight ahead and held my head high. I looked for an empty pew; I needed no preferential seating for this meeting. I just wanted it over with. As usual, the very front row had been left unoccupied, so my family and I, siblings included, sat there. It was wonderful to have their support. When I looked around, I didn't see Rev. Knighton. But the Voice had been right; it appeared all the members were there, including my contacts.

Deacon Murphy did not prolong the meeting. He told all the deacons and ministers to come forward and began the installation of Rev. Brown immediately. I was disappointed that Rev. Knighton had not come to support Rev. Brown. But to be perfectly honest, I was more disappointed that he was not present so that I could get my apology to him over. I hated the feeling that I would quite possibly be on my way back to the place I had just left less than twenty-four hours earlier. I tuned out the installation service and focused on how I would address the congregation.

Would I just point blank ask them to forgive me? The Voice had not instructed me on the procedure I should use. He had just made it clear that I'd better make it happen.

I decided that I would just tell them that my spirit had left my body and floated away to another world, a beautiful place where streets were paved with gold, a paradise of sorts.

I would then explain how disappointed I had been when I realized that my name had not been written in the Book of Righteousness. But on second thought, I concluded that I could not do that. No one would believe me, or forgive me for that matter. They would think I had absolutely lost my mind.

Then another thought entered my mind. Maybe I would be able to explain to them that I had talked to my father in another world and that he had told me why Rev. White had blackmailed him. I paused again. No, I couldn't say that either. The members would feel justified to send me to an insane asylum for sure.

I thought back to the time when I had first become aggressive toward the members. It was before my father passed away. I would have to choose my words carefully because their resentment was deep-rooted, and if they were going to accept my apology, I would have to come across as being truly genuine.

Bernadine Hopkins, in particular, would be a hard one to convince. She had gotten up to leave the moment I started to address the congregation at the special meeting prior to my collapse. I fully understood why she hadn't wanted to hear anything I had to say. Three years ago, she had chaired my father's Pastor's Anniversary Celebration. I disagreed with her decision to have the celebration immediately after morning worship and changed it to 5:00 p.m. in the evening. And if that weren't bad enough, I went over her authority and had the affair catered rather than allowing the kitchen committee to handle the food. The proverbial straw that broke the camel's back was my taking over the decorating of the fellowship hall and using my father's favorite colors of brown and gold, instead of going along with Bernadine's decision to use the bicentennial red, white, and blue. She had not spoken to me since that fiasco.

I glanced over at the Deacons. I had a long history of trying to control that board. Convincing them to forgive me would be the biggest challenge. Next, my gaze rested on Trustee Anderson, who looked away when he met my stare. He, too, would be a hard nut to crack. I remembered the day he had come by my father's office, smiling broadly and waving the estimates he had secured for the church renovations. His smile had soon faded when I learned that the remodeling would cost $20,000. I had risen out of my chair and harshly opposed.

Of course, my father had nodded in agreement. The color had drained out of Trustee Anderson's face when he heard my father agree with me.

“That was too much money, Trustee Anderson,” my father told him. “Thank you for your hard work, but the church can’t afford that kind of money. And anyway, I forgot to mention that I've decided to put the remodeling on hold for this year.”

Trustee Anderson walked out of his office and slammed the door so hard that I was certain that the glass panels would shatter. I felt confident that he blamed me for my father's change of mind, and to be totally honest, it was my fault. Come to think of it, it was my father’s fault as well. He knew there was not enough money in the treasure. He had used most the money in the church account to blackmailed Rev. White.

Needless to say, after Rev. Knighton became the pastor, he dismissed my meddling and the Deacons had agreed to proceed with the remodeling. My taking advantage of my father's position to run the church had come to a screeching halt, so my vendetta against Rev. Knighton had officially begun. Hence, the predicament I now found myself in, having to apologize for my despicable behavior.

I still had not decided exactly how I would address the congregation. If I told them the absolute truth, not only would they think I had fabricated a story but on the slim chance that they would believe me, they would not be willing to accept my apology and possibly even suggest having a special going away party to celebrate my going down the road to Hell, along with my father.

They had accepted it, but most still had not forgiven him for embezzling $100,000 from the church. They had always described my father and me as "two peas in a pod," so it would be highly unlikely for them to believe that I had changed in twenty-four hours. I took a deep breath and decided to speak from my heart.

When the installation was over, Deacon Murphy pronounced Rev. Brown as Pastor of Gastonia Church. I must admit that a part of me still wanted my brother in that position, but I had more pressing issues to contend with, one being how to get the members to accept my apology and another, how to get my Jerome appointed as Chair of the Deacon Board.

When the applause subsided and everyone had taken their seats, I asked Deacon Murphy if I could speak. He looked puzzled and hesitated, but I continued.

"Before you say no, I promised this will not be a repeat of the last meeting," I assured him.

"Well, if you promise," he said, reluctantly, "I guess it will be okay. We're so happy you're feeling better and back with us."

I nodded thinking "If I don't soon contact Rev. Knighton, this may well be the last you'll ever see of me."

I stood and cleared my throat. Facing the members was awkward for me. I was Tina Mae Black. Never before had I bowed down to anyone. When I opened my mouth to speak, I stared directly into Rev. White's eyes. For a moment, I lost my focus, thinking that he and my "father" were the cause of my being in this predicament. My "father" was on the road to Hell. I wondered how The Voice was going to punish Rev. White.

I surveyed the congregation and then began. "My behavior in our last meeting was not only irrational but also unruly. Although the McMann family established Gastonia Church, I now realize that no family can lay ownership to God's house. I have caused a great deal of trouble here ever since I can remember, and I am asking you to find enough compassion in your hearts to forgive me." At that point, my voice began to tremble, and I could hardly get out my last statement. "I promise you, I've changed."

The members stared in awe as I took my seat, tears streaming down my face. "Christians can be so forgiving," I thought as I heard an outburst of applause. I dared not look around because I would be sure to detect a facial expression that would indicate that not everyone had fallen for my performance.

Sitting down, I immediately remembered another hurdle. I would have to explain to Jerome about the $20,000 I dispersed among my contacts. It wouldn't be easy, but I would have to convince him to forgive me. When it became obvious that Rev. Knighton wasn't going to make an appearance at the meeting, I whispered to Jerome that I was ready to go home. I didn't want to hang around and have to exchange niceties after the meeting had ended, so we quietly left. My family followed us. When we reached the church grounds, Lisa embraced me and kissed me on the cheek.

"I'm so proud of you, Mom," she said. My siblings embraced me as well, and I couldn't help but wonder if this would be the last time I saw them. I needed an excuse to go downtown. I just had to get in touch with Rev. Knighton. Slowly, I pulled away from my family and I told Jerome that I needed to be alone before I went home. "I promise I'll be there within the hour," I promised. He reluctantly agreed and asked Bill to drop him and Lisa off.

Before I got into the car, Judy came up behind me with tearing rolling down her face. She said, "Tina Mae, you will always be my sister, and I love you," she began. "The day our father put me out, I told Junior to keep an eye on that old man. I never believed in him anyway. I will give you back the paper that I gave you at the church meeting, and I promise not to mention it until you're ready to sit down and discuss its contents with the family."

Judy had no idea that there was a very strong possibility that my secret would possibly never be revealed, unless she chose to reveal it, however. I was facing going on the road to Hell. How I wished I could explain everything to her, especially Jerome and Lisa. I wanted their help, but no rational person would accept such an outlandish story.

* * * *

The drive to the hotel where Rev. Knighton resided seemed long. The hotel lobby was empty, except for the blonde receptionist. I stood there patiently, waiting for her to end her personal phone call and became more and more agitated when I realized that she was obviously ignoring me.

I took some deep breaths and tried to remain calm. I didn't want to do or say anything that I would have to ask forgiveness for. I was already in a battle for my soul.

Suddenly, someone tapped me on the shoulder. I turned around quickly and was shocked to see Rev. Neil, the minister who had assisted Rev. Knighton with the Ordination Service at Gastonia church. "Hi there," he said, "Are you looking for someone?"

"Yes, as a matter of fact I am. I've been waiting here for a while trying to get someone's attention," I said, raising my voice so that the receptionist could hear me.

"Oh, Miss I apologize, but I was on an important business call," she lied. "Can I help you with something?"

"I'm looking for Rev. Knighton," I told her, unable to contain my agitation. "Can you ring his room and let him know Tina Mae Black is here to see him?"

"Rev. Knighton checked out last night," Rev. Neil chimed in before the receptionist could respond.

"Last night? Oh no, I must speak to him immediately. Do you know where I can reach him?"

"I thought I recognized you from last night's special church meeting," Rev. Neil continued. "Rev. Knighton has left town, but he promised to contact me later this evening."

"It is imperative that I speak to him before midnight! When he calls, please give him this number and ask him to call me. It is an absolute emergency."

Rev. Neil nodded and promised to relay the message. I had been hoping to talk to Rev. Knighton immediately, but if a promise of a call later is all I could get, then so be it. I walked out of the hotel lobby and headed for my car.

CHAPTER NINETEEN

On my way home, I had decided to go directly upstairs so that I could be alone with my thoughts. The moment I was alone in my bedroom, I took out my cell phone and checked for possible missed calls. There was none.

I didn't know if I just keep on the outfit I had worn to the meeting or change into some more comfortable. Then I decided that it really didn't matter if I didn't apologize to Rev. Wright. If the Voice summoned me back, my attire would be replaced with the black robe anyway. I decided that my time would be better spent doing something I had not done in quite some time.

I reached into the drawer of my nightstand, removed the Bible, and turned to my favorite scripture, Psalm 23. It was quite befitting because I was definitely going through the valley of the shadow of death. After reading, I continued watching the clock and waiting for the cell phone to ring. When I could no longer stand the suspense, I got angry with myself for not having the prescience of mind to request Rev. Neil's phone number so that I could call him to see if he had been able to give Rev. Knighton my message.

Then the thought came to me to try to reach him at the hotel number. I reached for the directory and started flipping through the yellow page. I thought I heard Jerome calling me. I quickly put the cell phone on silent and placed it in my purse.

I didn't know what to do; Rev. Knighton had an hour to call. I felt pretty certain that Rev. Neil had given him my message. Maybe his refusal to call was intentional. Maybe he hated me for what I had done to him over the past two years. Then I stopped myself. I was making myself crazy with all of the maybes. Sadly, I gave up waiting for his call.

The last time I looked at the clock it was 11:59 p.m. and Rev. Knighton had not called. Suddenly a strange sensation came upon me; I really can't explain how I felt it. I wanted to move but I couldn't. For a moment I don't know what happened. I thought I felt Jerome near me calling Tina Mae what's wrong honey. Before I could replied, I heard the Voice say, "I told you that you had until midnight to ask everyone for forgiveness, but you still have one more person to ask."

I opened my eyes and realized that I was standing in the same place as before reviewing my Book of Life and again my garments had been replaced by a black robe. It was unbelievable; my spirit had once again left my body.

"How did I get here?" I began with a barrage of questions. "What's going to happen to me? Why didn't Rev. Knighton call? Did Rev. Neil give him my message?"

I felt myself getting hysterical. I was at the point of shouting.

"You don't have to shout," said the Voice. "I hear you."

"You're not standing here facing damnation like me, so I don't expect you to understand how I feel," I told him. "Do something! You told me you had pity on me. My family thinks I'm back with them. What's going to happen when they discover I've had a relapse? Please give me more time to go back and find Rev. Knighton!"

"I gave you instructions and you refused to follow them. You can close the book now. There's nothing else for you to review."

My body began to tremble. I walked away from the book and turned toward the road while at the same time listening to my father's voice echoing "Don't come down this road!"

I decided then and there that I had to fight. The Voice sensed my hesitation.

"Remember who is in charge here!" he said. "You will abide by my will!"

CHAPTER TWENTY

My brother was a defense attorney, but this was no ordinary case. I could not depend upon him for assistance. I was not standing in a normal courtroom facing a judge. I was standing before the ultimate Judge, facing the fires of Hell where I would remain for eternity. In spite of the Voice's directive, I continued my protests.

"Let me make myself perfectly clear," I said, trying to sound calm. "There is something called fairness, even here! I don't deserve to spend eternity in Hell. I apologized to the congregation of Gastonia Church just like you asked me to and it is certainly not my fault that I was unable to get in touch with Rev. Knighton. Surely, you won't hold that against me. Please, won't you give me a second chance to go back to be with my family?"

The Voice did not respond, so I continued pleading my own case.

"Have you considered the shortcomings of the other members at Gastonia Church? Look at my Aunt Minnie, for instance. She knew my father was embezzling the church money, but she covered for him. And what about Rev. Johnson, who carried on an affair with my sister Rebecca for years? And just last week, Annie Marie Marble went to jail because she was selling drugs to some of the church members. And don't forget that beady-eyed Rev. White. He should be standing right here with me. After all, it's because of him and my father that I'm here in the first place!"

I paused. I really hated throwing others under the bus, but I was fighting for my life, and in such cases all is fair. But I was only wasting my breath. The Voice was all-knowing anyway!

After I finished speaking, the Voice responded. "You don't tell me how to do my job," he said. "Remember, I'm in charge here!"

He directed me to look to the right. Coming toward me was a man who resembled Rev. Neil, but that was not possible. I had just spoken to him this afternoon at the hotel.

"Try to relax, Tina Mae," he said. "I'm Rev. Neil. He was dressed in a white robe identical to one worn by others on the 'good road.' "When you saw me at the hotel this afternoon, I was preparing to leave to come here."

"Come here? But why are you here? Why did you tell me you were going to give Rev. Knighton my message if you were on your way here?"

"But I did give him your message."

"Well, if you gave Rev. Knighton the message, why didn't he call me? Did he say he would call?"

"No, I didn't say I would call," I heard a different voice say. When I turned toward the sound of that voice, I immediately recognized it as belonging to Rev. Knighton. He, too, wore a white robe and it became crystal clear that both Rev. Neil and Rev. Knighton were in this place together. A sense of doom began to overtake me. It was becoming less and less likely that I would be able to escape my impending fate.

"Is that you, Rev. Knighton?" I asked, afraid of the affirming response.

"Don't be afraid, Tina Mae," he said. "You didn't recognize me because when you come here, you are transformed." Transformed? I wondered what my new body looked like.

"I left Friday night after the Ordination because I had to have everything prepared before you and the others arrived."

"What others?" I asked, not sure what he was talking about.

"Don't you remember the Voice telling you that everyone travels the same road when they come here? Those wearing white robes are in good standing and will proceed through the Golden Gate. Others, like yourself, who are wearing black robes, are doomed to damnation."

"I know, I know, I know," I told him, not wanting him to repeat my fate. "You already explained that to me. But what I want to know is where all those people came from."

They were not visible, a long line of them, and they looked perfectly content in their white robes, walking toward the gate singing the same song that I now remembered that I had not heard before. Panic set in.

"Please calm down," the Voice continued. "I'll explain everything. On Friday night while we were at the special church meeting there was a terrible explosion."

"An explosion? Where?"

My family had not mentioned that to me, possibly because they felt I might get upset. Our town was close-knit, and I'm sure that I would know whoever was involved, so I listened intently.

"It occurred at Tamar Church on Lee Street."

I felt a huge lump form in my throat. Tamar Church was only two blocks over from Gastonia Church. Had I gone north to get downtown to see Rev. Knighton, I would have seen the devastation. The Voice could sense my obvious concern, so he continued.

"Because of that explosion, it took the paramedics half an hour to get you to the hospital when you collapsed at the meeting at Gastonia Church. Traffic was backed up for blocks by rescue vehicles and people trying to get to the church to see if their loved ones were safe."

I could hardly believe what I was hearing. I knew many of the members of Tamar Church and now found myself wondering who had survived the disaster.

"But what on earth caused the explosion? I asked him.

"It was a gas leak," he said. "We're not sure what sparked the fire, but everyone at the church for concert choir rehearsal perished in the fire. Pastor Gibson and his wife tried to get everyone out, but the fire spread so quickly that they all were trapped."

I stood in awe. That concert choir was made up of all ages and all ethnicities. And many of the members had family connections.

"But why on earth were Rev. Gibson and his wife at the rehearsal anyway?" I thought. He was such a busy pastor and, from what I had been told by one of his members, he left the associates in charge of overseeing the various ministries. But he had always taken special interest in his choirs. So maybe that explained his presence at the church. Then I remembered what Rev. Gibson had said to me years earlier, when I was only ten. He had warned me not to be a goat dressed in a black robe. I looked down at myself and tears spilled over and ran down my cheeks.

"I know many of these people," I said. "They used to be in the concert choir at Gastonia Church." Then I paused. I was not about to reveal out how my father and I mistreated them, causing them to leave the ministry and go to Tamar Church. As I thought about it, we were partly to blame for their deaths. Had they remained at Gastonia

Church, they would not have been at Tamar Church when the explosion occurred.

I could not get the thought out of my head. I reminisced about all I had done to cause those former Gastonia Church members to feel that they had to leave the church. I opposed them at times just for the sake of opposition, knowing that my father would go along with whatever decisions I made.

Now, I felt genuinely sorry. I desired an opportunity to ask for their forgiveness, but I knew it was too late. They were dressed in white, and I, the infamous black. I was doomed!

I looked back at Rev. Knighton and asked, "You knew I had been here before, didn't you?"

"Yes, I did. Rev. Neil, my assistant, and I are from here. That's why I asked him to come and assist me at the Ordination Service at Gastonia Church the other night. We only pastored for two years because we were both on assignment. The Voice wanted Gastonia Church and Greater Matthew, Rev. Neil's ministry, to be churches after God's own heart. Families controlled both churches and the pastors had scattered the flocks. Therefore, the Voice had sent Rev. Neil and me to make sure the turmoil ceased in those churches."

"Okay, so Rev. Knighton, can you tell me why The Voice has brought me back here?

"Tina Mae, The Voice is the only one who will answer that question."

"Why did you send me back to ask Rev. Knighton for forgiveness when you knew all along that he would be here?"

I asked the Voice.

The Voice did not answer.

"I think I've figured it out. You asked me to apologize to Rev. Knighton. Well, he's right here, so all I have to do now is apologize and then I can be on my way back to my family."

"Oh no, it is not that simple," The Voice spoke up. "Well, anyway, I don't want to discuss Gastonia Church or anything else for that matter. I just want to go back!"

"Tina Mae, please understand what The Voice is trying to explain to you. You wanted to elect your brother Bill as the Pastor of Gastonia Church and that complicated everything. That secret plan of yours just interfered with the work that I had been assigned to do. I had been instructed to mentor Rev. Brown, but I had to be subtle in my approach. That is why I took up residence at the hotel where he ate lunch every day. The plan was for me to pastor Gastonia Church for two years while I prepared him to take the reins.

"Your secret plan interfered with the one I sent," The Voice thundered." "When you arrived here, I explained, that the man at the Golden Gate was a very important person to me. You had no idea that the person I was referring to was Rev. Knighton. You touched my anointed and sought to do my prophet harm. And that, my daughter, is why you are here!"

My body began to tremble. My punishment would last for eternity. There was no way of escape. Or was there?

I looked over at Rev. Knighton, tears were rolling down my face. "I – I – didn't know who you were," I told him, hoping his compassion would set in. "Please forgive me and talk to The Voice. You have the power to save me from this awful fate. Please, speak to him on my behalf."

"Tina Mae, I've already done what I can do for you. I've known about this all along. That's why on Friday morning, I went into the sanctuary and prayed for you. I asked for forgiveness on your behalf and now it is up to The Voice to answer my prayer to save you."

I sobbed as I fell to my knees. My prayer was short, but fervent. "Please, allow me to go back to my family. I am a changed person. Honor the prayer request of Rev. Knighton, Please!"

The Voice's response came suddenly. "From this experience, you should remember to listen to wise counsel. You never know who has been sent to have authority over you."

"But what about Rev. Knighton's prayer?" I asked, afraid of The Voice's response.

He paused for a moment. "Rev. Knighton prayed. Now it's up to me to answer his prayer."

He paused again, as if reflecting on my complete past and then responded, "I want you to get up off your knees. Rev. Knighton and Rev. Neil will escort you to your destination."

"My destination?" I asked, fearing the worst. "Please tell me you're not sending me to Hell!" I sobbed. "What about all the prayers? And what about the forgiveness that you've always stressed for believers?"

I had to make a last ditch effort to save myself. I was not about to go down without a fight. In obedience, Rev. Knighton and Rev. Neil came and stood in front of me, each taking hold of an arm. I wrestled with all that was in me, trying to get loose from their grips. I began screaming to the top of my lungs. I felt that I was on my way to an eternal prison for a crime I had not committed. I closed my eyes tightly, not daring to look down the road for fear of what I might see. With each step, the sound of The Voice's echo was fading. I did, however, manage to hear him say,

"Remember, I'll be watching you." Then there was total silence.

"But Please!" I began to plead, but Rev. Knighton stopped me.

"It's useless to speak to him now," he said. "He won't hear you."

Suddenly, a strong wind came from the east. I held on tightly to Rev. Knighton and Rev. Neil. When it had subsided, I looked down and realized we were standing on a street paved with gold. I didn't quite understand what was happening, but I didn't dare ask any questions. I grabbed on that ounce of hope that this just might turn out in my favor. But then again, maybe The Voice was just giving me a small glimpse of what I would be missing by not being in Heaven.

Suddenly, I heard someone calling my name softly. I knew it wasn't Rev. Knighton or Rev. Neil; the voice was familiar. I stopped walking and turned abruptly to Rev. Knighton.

"Did you hear that?" I asked him. "Someone is calling me."

"I didn't hear anything," he said, turning his head as if trying to hear.

Then I heard my name again; the sound was getting closer. I wondered if it could be my imagination, since I wanted out of this situation so badly. Rev. Knighton nudged me forward and we continued to walk. But once again I heard my name, this time much louder. I pulled away from my escorts so that I could walk toward the sound. When they stood still and did not try to follow me, I looked over my shoulder just as Rev. Knighton said, "This is as far as we go with you, Tina Mae." Then they walked away. I was frightened out of my wits, so I began pleading again, tears flowing down my face.

"Please don't leave me here alone," I begged, but they never turned around. I screamed like a frightened child whose mother had disappeared. Thick fog engulfed me, and I could hardly see my way. I did, however, hear Rev. Knighton's voice echoing "Walk straight ahead, Tina Mae. Think positive, and your faith will lead you to your destination."

"Rev. Knighton, please come back!" I yelled toward the sound of his echo. "I don't want to go on that road. Hell is not my home."

But he didn't answer. So I continued with measured steps. Suddenly, the movement of my body was in slow motion. I felt as if I was being carried along without any effort on my part. Then I heard my name again; this time it was loud and clear and I recognized the voice. It was Jerome.

"Honey, is that you?" I asked, barely able to restrain my joy.

"Yes, of course it's me, Tina Mae. Why are you asking that?"

"They are trying to direct me to that road, Jerome, and I don't want to go on that road!"

"Tina Mae, Tina Mae, wake up, honey. You're dreaming," he said shaking me gently. I was in a daze. Slowly I opened my eyes.

"Are you okay? That dream must have been something terrible. What road are you talking about?"

"That road over there."

"Tina Mae, you're okay now. Just look around. See, you're right here at home with me."

My eyes widened. I surveyed the room to see if I were, in fact, in my own home. I looked down at the beige carpet and to the left at my nightstand. Everything was in place. My comforter and pillows, my furniture, my what-nots on the dresser - everything looked familiar. I was in my own bedroom. I gave myself a tight squeeze.

"I'm back," I yelled. "I'm not going on that road." Jerome looked at me strangely and took me into his arms.

"Honey, what do you mean you're back? And what road are you talking about? Are you okay?"

I held on to my husband for dear life and whispered, "Yes, I'm okay, but please just hold me!"

I rested in Jerome's arms for quite some time. He explained to me that I had been sleeping soundly for a while, so long in fact, that he had become worried. But then he had heard me screaming in my sleep and that is when he had come to awaken me.

"It's okay now," he reassured me. "You've just had a bad dream."

With that, I snuggled up to Jerome even more closely and vowed to be the best person I could be, now and forever. I had learned my lesson. The Voice had given me another chance, and I would be eternally grateful. Thank God, Hell was not my home."

www.ingramcontent.com/pod-product-compliance
Lightning Source LLC
Chambersburg PA
CBHW020848090426
42736CB00008B/285

* 9 7 8 0 6 9 2 4 9 6 1 3 8 *